ROSSEN TO THE RESCUE

ROSSEN

TO THE

RESCUE

Secrets to Avoiding Scams, Everyday Dangers, and Major Catastrophes

JEFF ROSSEN

FLATIRON
BOOKS
NEW YORK

www.flatironbooks.com

Book design by Richard Oriolo

The Library of Congress Cataloging-in-Publication Data is available upon request.

ISBN 978-1-250-11943-8 (hardcover)
ISBN 978-1-250-11944-5 (ebook)

Our books may be purchased in bulk for promotional, educational, or business use. Please contact your local bookseller or the Macmillan Corporate and Premium Sales Department at 1-800-221-7945, extension 5442, or by email at MacmillanSpecialMarkets@macmillan.com.

First Edition: October 2017

10   9   8   7   6   5   4   3   2   1

To Danielle, my true soul mate, who always comes to my rescue.

And to my kids, Skyler, Sloane, and Blake . . .

The best experiments of my life.

CONTENTS

CONTENTS

CONTENTS

CONTENTS

9. A SHOCKING CONCLUSION ◎ 221

INTRODUCTION

DO YOU KNOW HOW TO survive a plane crash? How to spot bedbugs? What if someone breaks into your home? What if a contractor is trying to rip you off?

Most of us don't know any of this stuff. And most of us don't even consider it. It's human nature. Our brain makes a simple assumption: Because nothing disastrous happened yesterday, nothing disastrous will happen tomorrow.

Yet there's one tiny problem with this logic. Disasters *do* happen. They happen to good people. For the past several years, I've crisscrossed the country to research the surprising ways our luck can turn on a dime, how to respond in every kind of emergency, how to sniff out hidden dangers, and how to save you cash.

That's my mission with Rossen Reports. As the national investigative correspondent for NBC's *Today* show, I've spent years putting myself into the shoes of . . . well, *you*. I try to solve your problems. I consult with the nation's top experts on earthquakes, webcam predators, fake rubies, and everything from train safety to rigged carnival games. My goal is to give you tips, strategies, and takeaways that are actually useful—not some theoretical mumbo jumbo.

I also believe in learning by doing. And I believe in putting my money where my mouth is. So, to find out how to survive an avalanche, I actually buried myself alive. (Spoiler alert: I got out.) I was stranded at sea to show you how to survive, I trapped myself in a car and drove through a flood (my wife was so thrilled), and I walked across hot coals barefoot. This book will take you inside my dramatic experiments and the stuff I couldn't show you on TV. I'm also getting super personal here. Revealing things about my own life I've never shared before. Some of it is emotional. A lot of it is embarrassing. But since you bought this book, you are now my friend. And friends get full access.

I began working on this book, in a sense, when I was eleven years old. My mom took me to a mall on Long Island and we saw a man sitting behind a desk doing a live radio show. He was surrounded by speakers. He was balding, overweight, and he spoke into a microphone. A crowd of maybe ten people circled around him, mesmerized. I turned to my mom. "I want to be him someday. I want to do that."

And, in fact, I *did* turn into that guy. (At the very least, I certainly lost some hair and gained some weight.) I weaseled my way into a college radio station at the age of thirteen, doing whatever odd jobs they would give me, fascinated by the DJ flipping switches and touching buttons. I asked him question after question while he played a college mix of reggae and jazz and pop and classical. *What's that button do? How do you change the sound mix?*

In high school, I somehow talked my way into an internship at ABC Radio. (Not unrelated: Girls weren't exactly banging down my door. I like to think it was my orange neon shorts, not my personality.) But it finally paid off. It all led to a real reporting job at the ABC affiliate in Syracuse while I was still a full-time college student. After graduation I moved to Detroit, then to New York, and then, ultimately, to NBC News. From the very beginning, I was fascinated by two core questions: *How can I help people?* And *How do I cut through the crap?*

That's what this book is all about. Real stuff. Real people. Sometimes the advice can save your life, sometimes it can save you cash, and sometimes it can save you some calories. There is one bit of advice, however, that you will never hear: *Don't panic.*

I HATE that phrase. Put it into the *junk* folder. Not only is the advice clichéd, it's just stupid. Because in a life-threatening situation, you *will* panic. It's unavoidable. I know this because I constantly throw myself into these harrowing scenarios and, every time, I panic. The human body has a fight-or-flight mechanism that is designed to unleash at times of anxiety. Panic is in our bones. It's better to just *know* that you will panic, accept it, and factor it into your plan.

Now, you might have a very reasonable question: Okay, so if I can't avoid panicking, then what *can* I do?

You can learn some tricks, and dramatically boost your odds of survival, from natural disasters to crooked contractors. Let's say, for example, a "mold inspector" visits your house and slaps you with a $700 bill. Should you pay? Is he legit? This book gives you some simple solutions. There are a few buzzwords you can say, a few things you can do, to send a message that's crystal clear—*Mess with the next guy, not me.*

Here's the honest truth: When I'm not on TV, I'm just the guy whose toilet broke, and needs to find a plumber to fix it. Or the guy whose car got a flat tire. Or the guy who's worried about the safety of his kids. Or the guy who is helping his mother fight cancer, hugging and hoping and praying. I'm just a *guy*. That's where all these stories come from—my random questions about how to spot hidden dangers, how to stay safe, and how to sniff out a scam.

And I've learned a few things. After years of near-death experiences, tests in laboratories, interviews with experts, and more experiments than I can possibly count, I want to share what I've learned with you.

It just might save your life.

1

PROTECTING
YOUR HOME

WE THINK OF OUR HOMES as safe. A place to unwind, relax, and recharge. Yet if we're not careful . . .

- How to Survive a Home Invasion
- How to Spot Hidden Mold
- Why Your New House May Catch Fire
- You Probably Don't Have a Fire Escape Plan
- Help! I'm Locked Out!
- When the Bottom Falls Out . . . Literally
- Surviving Mother Nature
- Secret Spies Inside Your Bedroom

How to Survive a Home Invasion

1986. Midnight. I was ten years old, sound asleep in my bedroom. My brother was asleep in his room, and my parents asleep in theirs.

Bang. Bang. Bang.

The sound woke me up.

Bang. Bang. Bang.

The sound came from downstairs. It didn't sound like my father or a friend or a neighbor who came to borrow a cup of sugar. The sound was terrifying. Alien.

Bang. Bang. Bang.

I pulled the covers close to me. I was paralyzed—my family had never discussed a "safety plan" in case of a home invasion, and I didn't know what to do. I stayed frozen in my bedroom.

My father, however, did not stay frozen.

I heard my parents' bedroom door swing open, and my father raced from his room and flicked on the lights. He suddenly transformed into an action-movie hero.

"We're home and I have a bat!" my father screamed, charging downstairs. He jumped seven stairs at a time, headlong into the face of danger. "I have a bat!" he yelled again.

My dad's heroics worked. He scared the would-be robber away and, as we crept downstairs into the kitchen, I saw something terrifying. The *bang, bang, bang* had come from a thief kicking the dead bolt on our back door. The lock was busted. The door frame was cracked. One more kick and he would have been inside, and then . . . who knows what. It had been raining that night, and when I looked outside I could see footprints in the lawn. I can still see those footprints. And I still have a lingering fear of home invasions; even when I travel, I avoid first-floor hotel rooms.

The statistics provide little comfort, as home invasions are more common than you might think—they happen nearly 50,000 times a year, or 135 every day. No one is immune. In recent years, Sandra Bullock, Ray Allen, and even the Kennedy family had their homes violated.

If the rich and famous are vulnerable—even with their fancy security systems—all of us are. Anyone can find themselves in the predicament like Susan Dawson from Fountain Hills, Arizona, who was the victim of a home invasion. Her story is chilling. She saw an intruder in her home, and screamed, "Oh my gosh, who are you?!" and then he ran across the room and punched her in the nose. Then he tied her up.

"I lay there, and he kept going through the bedroom, looking for stuff," Susan told me. While tied up she kept asking herself, *How is he going to kill me?*

Susan lived to tell the tale. And she's proof that there are, thankfully, a few things you can do to maximize your chances of making it out alive. For guidance, I spoke to Wallace Zeins, a former NYPD detective, and a hostage negotiator with twenty-two years of experience. (Zeins has a tough, intense stare—this is not a guy you want to play in a poker tournament.)

"So if I hear a noise in my home, what do I do?" I ask him.

"Real simple. A lot of people don't have alarms, they're very expensive. So . . . instead of leaving your car keys downstairs, leave them on your night table."

His advice is simple, easy, and smart. If you hear a noise downstairs, just click the car alarm, and that should frighten the intruder, meaning you won't have to race downstairs like my father. Intruders hate the attention. Noise is the enemy.

There's another thing you can do, and it costs less than a dollar. For about ninety-nine cents, you can buy a tiny alarm called a "window alert." You just stick it on a window or a door, and if an intruder opens it, the sensors get separated and it emits a loud, piercing alarm.

And in that vein, there are plenty of new, affordable gadgets that work with your smartphone where you get an alert right away when someone is in your home. With the Canary home security system, for example, a live video feed shows you their every move, and you can even call police with the touch of a button. Best part? The gadgets record everything.

So what happens if, worst case, you are captured like Susan Dawson? There's one key course of action: cooperation. If they ask where the money is, you tell them. If they ask where the jewelry is, you tell them. You can always get more cash or sapphires; you can never get a new heartbeat. "Treat them like royalty," advises Zeins. This is exactly what Susan Dawson did, and this is why she's still alive.

It pays to play it safe and take these precautions. It's also worth remembering that these guidelines—like all the guidelines in this book—are just that, *guidelines,* and not hard and fast rules. In any life-and-death situation, you need to keep your head on a swivel and be prepared to improvise. My dad did not technically play things by the book, but he may have saved our lives. Then again, in 1986, we didn't have remote-controlled car alarms or ninety-nine-cent window alerts. Our "home alarm" was a baseball bat and a whopping dose of courage. (Thanks again, Dad.) But now we do have those technologies—let's use them.

How to Spot Hidden Mold

My kids are young, so sippy cups are my life. I have what seems like every color, every shape, every style. I clean them after every use. But then I saw something that rocked my sippy little world.

A woman snapped a photo of her son's sippy cup and it went viral. From the outside the cup looked normal. Clean. Shiny. When you peel open the lid, however, you can see dark clumps of mold that look like a mix of vomit, feces, and rotten cheese. Lovely. The photos freaked out the parenting community, including me.

So that got me thinking . . . how much mold is lurking in *my* home?

I like to think my family is tidy. We regularly scrub our counters, sweep, mop, vacuum, even dust. (Okay, maybe "regular dusting" is a stretch. But we do own a feather-duster. I think.) To put my own home to the test, I invite a certified mold inspector, Matt Waletzke, to expose my moldy laundry.

Waletzke ping-pongs through my apartment, back and forth, from room to room, opening cabinet doors and peering underneath furniture. *(Why did I agree to this?)* He points a handheld contraption that looks straight out of *Star Trek*, with a tiny monitor that analyzes what's lurking under my sink.

I feel good about the kitchen. It's clean . . . and then he opens the cabinet door under the sink.

"You find anything?" I ask.

"I did. Under here, where you keep all of your cleaning products." He points to some dark stains underneath the bottles of (ironically) disinfectant. "There's a plumbing leak here, which is causing some moisture and some mold growth." If left unchecked, it could become a bigger problem.

Then he stands up and points to my sink, which, if I do say so myself, looks *spotless*. I take pride in a clean kitchen and a clean sink. He holds up a little metal tray that holds our sponge. "Down in this little tray here, there's a lot of black growth. . . ."

Are you kidding me? Then it dawns on me . . . this is the very tray that holds the sponge. The sponge is what I use to clean the dishes. The dishes are used to eat food. The food goes in my body.

"And then one thing a lot of people don't know about is underneath the refrigerator," the inspector says. "Under here there's a drip pan."

A refrigerator has a "drip pan"? No one told me about drip pans. They don't teach you that in Grown-Up 101. Waletzke bends to his knees, reaches under the fridge, and pulls out a large tray. The tray oozes with dark liquids and slime and murky sauces. I avert my eyes, horrified.

"That is hideous!" I cry out.

"Yeah," he agrees, not even bothering to sugarcoat it. "This is all mold and bacterial growth that's built up over time."

"I never even knew this was here." I'm still shell-shocked.

"Most people don't." He adds that you can avoid this problem by cleaning the drip pan once or twice a month. "That's enough to take care of it."

Again I force myself to look at the brown sewage-looking water inside the pan. "This is the kind of stuff that can make you sick, if it's left untreated?"

"It could."

He heads to the washing machine, and when he opens the door

I breathe a sigh of relief. *Phew.* It's clean. Then he peels back the rubber liner from the door . . . and reveals dark smudges and streaks of mold. So. Damn. Gross. "How dangerous is this?"

"That could be dangerous if it gets airborne and you're breathing it."

Of course I didn't know any of that . . . so I was putting my kids at risk without even realizing it.

\ \ \ \ | / / /

BIG TIP HERE: Front-loading washers are often teeming with bacteria. Pull back the rubber lining around the door and wipe it down with a paper towel between washes. To help prevent mold entirely, keep the door cracked open so air can get in when you're not using it. Then the moisture won't build and the mold can't grow.

/ / / | | \ \ \

And now for the coup de grace: my bathroom. He steps into my shower, pokes around the shampoo and conditioner bottles, and then motions for me to step inside the shower. We're now both standing inside my small shower. Just two grown men in the shower, face-to-face, having a conversation about mold.

"This is not weird at all," I say, and he laughs a little.

Waletzke holds up the shampoo bottles. "You and your wife have a lot of products in here, and sometimes, when you don't use them all the time, you don't notice the buildup."

I look closer. At the bottom of the bottle is a thick, black layer of grime. *Ew.* "Ugh, that's disgusting," I say, by way of scientific analysis.

He points to more bottles, more hair products, and more dark stains. My entire shower is a cesspool.

Waletzke points to another bottle, this one with a tag at the bottom. "You can see the mold growth on the tag. Mold loves paper like that."

"So I should rip the stickers off, at the very least?"

"At the very least," he agrees, "especially in the shower."

He finds more cheery news in the bathtub. Every night, before my kids go to bed, I give them a bath. I use a blue plastic pail to scoop water on their heads. Waletzke inspects this blue pail . . . and finds an unholy amount of dark slime.

"And this is the pail that I use . . . every night to pour over my kids heads when I wash their hair," I say, staring at the slime. "That's scary."

"It is," he says grimly.

"Hey, thanks so much for coming by, by the way."

"Anytime." We shake hands.

"Never come over again," I say, laughing, and he laughs, too, but I wasn't really joking.

KEY TAKEAWAY: Scrub the places you *don't* think need scrubbing. Clean your drip pan. And if you see something that looks like mold, it might be worth it to call a professional mold inspector.

(But can you actually *trust* these mold inspectors? Glad you asked—before you call one, be sure you read pages 84–88.)

Why Your New House May Catch Fire

Every year, thousands of people are killed in house fires. Usually there's very little time to escape—just a few minutes, tops. And it seems like the problem is getting worse. I'm no fire marshal, but it sure feels like homes are burning faster than they used to when I was a kid. Are today's homes actually *more* flammable than the ones from the old days?

I decide to channel my inner pyromaniac to create a little experiment. In a fire lab in Chicago, a team constructs two mini "homes" and builds them side by side. The first room is a throwback to the seventies or eighties, the way homes used to be built, and is decorated with older furniture. The coffee table is made from real wood. The couch is made from natural fabrics.

The second room? It looks a lot like, well, the way your own home probably looks now. It has modern furniture and synthetic fibers—synthetic curtains, a synthetic couch, even synthetic fibers in the coffee table.

It's time for the fire. I put on a hard hat and safety goggles—(not the sexiest look, but it keeps us safe)—and watch them light that eighties house. I stand inside the old room with John Drengenberg, a consumer safety director at Underwriters Laboratories. The pros start a fire on the old couch, and a pillow begins to gently burn. I brace myself for a dramatic flame and an explosion, but instead . . . just a few licks of fire. I wait for a minute—still just a small flicker. Two minutes—it has barely spread. Three, four, five minutes . . . no fiery inferno, no scorching flames.

Ten minutes: the fire is still contained to the couch.

Fifteen minutes: Yep, still on the couch.

Twenty-five minutes: The fire still hasn't left the couch. Theoretically, I had time to calmly sit down on the floor and watch an entire episode of *Seinfeld*. (Note to reader: Do NOT watch an entire episode of *Seinfeld* while your home is burning around you.) The fire still hasn't spread to the coffee table, it hasn't reached the plant, and the puffs of black smoke, while not exactly pleasant, are not yet overpowering.

Finally the rest of the room gets engulfed by the flames, and I scamper out the door to safety. It took thirty *minutes* for that eighties house to burn. Of course it's still a very dangerous situation, but it allows plenty of time for you and your family to get to safety.

How about the modern room?

The pros start the fire in the same place—on the synthetic couch.

Whoooooosh! Instantly the flames dance higher and higher, quickly spreading across the couch. "The backing of your carpet is synthetic, your drapes are synthetic, the couch, the pillows are synthetic," says Drengenberg, the safety director. "They burn hotter and faster than natural materials do."

Do they ever. Seconds later the entire couch is consumed by flames. It jumps to the lamp and the end table. And now I'm having a hard time breathing—the black smoke has slithered into my throat, and even though this is a highly controlled lab, I feel a quick shard of fear. Smoke does that to you.

Two minutes and twenty seconds: the chair is on fire.

Two minutes and forty seconds: the coffee table is on fire.

Like an idiot I'm still standing in the room, and now the roof is on fire.

"Should we leave?!" I ask Drengenberg, hoping that my voice doesn't sound completely panicked.

"Yeah, let's get out of here," he says, nodding.

We both sprint through the doorway . . . and the modern room is now a heap of ashes.

So for those of you scoring at home: It took less than three minutes for the modern room to burn, and thirty minutes for that old room. It turns out this isn't an aberration. Research shows that in the 1980s, you had an average of seventeen minutes to escape a burning home. Today? Only three to four minutes. One big reason is synthetic fiber, explains Drengenberg. "It's the way homes are furnished today. There's no getting away from that."

This feels so profoundly unfair. As civilization marches forward and technology improves, we like to imagine that things get *better* with time. Computers are faster. Cars are safer. Yet, when it comes to our homes and fire safety, things have actually taken a step backward.

So why build furniture with flammable synthetics? Yep, it's cheaper. Cheaper for the manufacturer and, therefore, cheaper for us to buy. There's not as much real wood. It's stuff that *looks* like wood. So we're all part of the problem. We demand more affordable furniture, and the industry has given us what we want. (But is asking for affordable, nonflammable furniture really too much to ask?)

The one silver lining is that, according to the National Association of Home Builders, the new building codes actually make the houses safer overall, when you consider other risk factors such as the chance of collapse. And the American Home Furnishings Alliance, aware of the problem, supports a federal flammability standard for upholstered furniture . . . but only if the product changes are safe, effective, and affordable.

I wish I could tell you to avoid synthetic furniture and bedding altogether, but that's nearly impossible, as it's everywhere. So there are two key takeaways:

1) If a fire strikes, don't dawdle. "When your smoke alarm goes off you don't have time to look around to get your wedding pictures," advises Drengenberg. Get out quick.

2) Stick to your fire escape plan.

You have a fire escape plan, right? That leads us to . . .

You Probably Don't Have a Fire Escape Plan

Every few months, the fire marshal comes to my office at 30 Rock to give the obligatory fire-safety speech. Some real talk: I've been the guy falling asleep during this speech. Most of us have. I used to zone out and think about my next meeting, or my kid's upcoming birthday, or fantasize about that second cup of coffee.

It's human nature. Most of us don't really take "fire safety" seriously until it's far too late. The numbers back this up: a whopping 82 percent of families have never practiced a fire-safety drill, and 52 percent have never even discussed fire safety with their kids. Most of us think, "I know my house, I could get out in an emergency." After all, I get up to go to the bathroom in the pitch-black. I can do it with my eyes closed. So, it seems simple, right? *Step 1. Look for the flames. Step 2. Run in the opposite direction.*

But it's not that simple.

To demonstrate just how easy it is to get disoriented without a good plan, we put a Connecticut family through the ultimate fire drill, even pumping in smoke machines and fake flames. They seemed confident.

"Do you guys have a fire plan as a family?" I ask them.

"We do not," says the mom.

"If there's a fire, do you think you can get out?"

"I think we could, yeah," says the dad.

"No big deal?" I ask.

"Eh, no, I guess it's easy to get out," says the son.

We send the family upstairs to bed, then wait for them to settle in. Once the kids drift off to sleep, and in the pitch-black of night, we unleash the smoke. We're watching a live feed on infrared cameras.

"Hit the smoke alarm!" I tell the team. So they push the smoke alarm. *BEEP! BEEP! BEEP!*

Instantly the mom and dad stand up and head for the hallway.

Mistake #1. "In a real fire, there are superheated gases up high [in the air]," says Ryan O'Donnell, CEO of BullEx, a fire-safety company. "A couple of breaths there, they'd be all done."

I check in on the kids—they scramble from their beds and head for the bedroom door . . . where they open it right up.

Mistake #2. "There could have been a large body of fire right on the other side of that door," explains O'Donnell. "That's a critical mistake. They should have taken the time to feel the door."

Smoke fills the house. Of course the flames aren't real—the family knows they're just on a video screen—but they are still disoriented and blinded. "Where are you?!" the mom calls out to the kids. They can barely see the stairs, stumbling and fumbling.

Eventually—too slowly—they make their way down to the front door . . . a way out. But then the mom makes one last mistake. A big one.

"I'm gonna get the dog," the mom says. She goes back inside the house.

"You never want to pass an exit," says O'Donnell. "Especially to go deeper into the fire. This is not survivable." (No matter how much you love your dog. Sorry, Scraps.)

This experiment scared me straight, and since then I've had multiple talks with my own kids about our fire escape plan. We practice it. The experts say it's critical to practice your plan while you're awake and alert, training our brains for when a real emergency strikes.

Think of it like sports: Whether it's baseball or soccer or tennis, athletes practice the same drill again and again until it becomes second nature, creating muscle memory, and preparing their bodies for decisive action when the game is actually on the line. If athletes do this for something as silly as tossing leather balls in a basket, why not take the same approach for saving the lives of your family?

I've now embraced this mind-set. I work in a New York City skyscraper, so I speak with my team all the time—*What would you do if the east side of the building is on fire? The west side? Which stairs do you use?* At home my family practiced the fire drill, and my kids were astonished to find they don't need to leave through the front door. There are other exits—ones they don't normally use. Seems obvious to us adults, but to kids, the front door is how they come in every day. What if we hadn't shown them, and they just assumed it's the front door or bust? Now they know that if there's a fire, they have a second avenue for escape.

I'm also now more careful about checking the smoke detectors once a month, replacing the batteries twice a year, and keeping a fire extinguisher by the kitchen.

To help you create a fire escape plan, the American Red Cross has a handy worksheet on its website. The statistics are grim: In 2015 alone, there were nearly 488,000 structure fires, resulting in 2,800 deaths. According to the American Red Cross, every two and a half hours someone is killed in a home fire. So why toss the dice?

Help! I'm Locked Out!

It's happened to you. It's happened to me. And it's frustrating. You lock your keys inside the house—just a boneheaded mistake—and now you're standing outside, desperate, maybe freezing cold, and you're forced to call an emergency locksmith.

But I had a hunch: Don't the locksmiths *know* that we're desperate? Are they jacking up their fees to exploit our vulnerability? According to the Better Business Bureau, some "rogue locksmiths" are leaving many consumers out in the cold. So I hatched a little experiment. In 2011, my team rented a suburban house as our "laboratory," and we hired a licensed locksmith, Jerry Giamanco, to install some simple locks on a door. These are basic locks, according to our expert, and they should only take a few seconds to crack. We watch him pick the lock in just seconds. Easy. Giamanco says the job should cost around one hundred bucks.

But what would other locksmiths do?

Ada, my trusty NBC producer, purposely locks herself outside.

With the rest of our production team, I stay out of sight in a secret control room.

"I'm locked out of the house," Ada tells a locksmith over the phone, "and I need someone to help me get back in!"

She calls a second locksmith. Then a third. She eventually calls *eight* locksmiths to see how they would respond. All eight of these locksmiths are the kind you see in ads around town, usually claiming "low prices" and 24-hour service.

Soon the first one arrives.

"I'm so glad you finally got here!" says Ada, really showing her acting chops.

The first one picks the lock and only charges $97. Nice! This is what our expert said it should cost—not everyone's a crook.

Then the second one arrives.

"Hi!" says Ada, feigning a note of desperation. "I thought you'd never get here."

This particular locksmith, like many, touts a "$15 service fee." But when he gets to the door . . .

"It's a hundred dollars *and* the fifteen-dollar service fee," the locksmith says. Instead of *picking* the lock—what our expert said every legit locksmith should do—he tries to pry the door open with a board. But that doesn't work. So this "expert" pulls out a pair of pliers and rips off the doorknob.

Now, in fairness to the locksmith, that's exactly what I would do if I needed to break in—I would rip off the doorknob. But then again, I am not a licensed locksmith. The math is starting to add up: We're on the hook for the $15 service fee, the $100 base fee, plus a brand-new lock and doorknob. Total price: $223.

And here's the real crazy thing: In most states, locksmiths don't have to go through background checks or be licensed. (Yep, this means that with just a little bit of Internet advertising and a whole lot of BS, you, too, can call yourself a professional locksmith.)

Once again, Giamanco installs a fresh lock and once again, Ada calls a locksmith. And once again, a contractor shows up at the door. This one *immediately brings out a drill*. He doesn't even try to pick the lock! He barely glances at it. And since he destroyed the old lock with his drill, oh, hey, whattya know! He just happens to have a new one that he can sell Ada for $265. I pop out from my hiding place and confront the guy.

"You didn't even try to pick the lock!" I tell him.

"Because I'm *experienced*," he says. "That's what I do."

Incredulous, I let him continue.

"You don't pick locks," the man says. "In the movies they pick locks. You can't pick a lock."

The movies, huh? Then how was our expert able to pick the lock in *seconds*?

He leaves, we reset the experiment, and the next guy charges $275 to drill the lock . . . and then $225 for a new lock. We've sailed to $500 before he even starts to do any work. Then he begins to drill. Final price? $635, or about the cost of some laptops.

"It's horrible!" Jerry Giamanco says, devastated by his colleagues' deception. "That's ridiculous. It's a hundred-dollar job."

Oh, but it gets better. This "professional" locksmith says his credit-card machine isn't working, so he wants it all in cash.

"I don't have $635 in cash," says Ada.

"Maybe we could go to the bank or something?" asks the locksmith.

"The bank?" Ada asks.

When Ada resists, the locksmith calls his boss to ask for instructions. When he gets off the phone he tells Ada, "$685."

Yep, the price has gone *up*.

"I don't carry over $600 in cash on me," says Ada, now speaking to the locksmith's boss. "Tell him to take me to the ATM and then drive me back home? I don't know."

Now, in this case, Ada knows that she's protected with cameras and a news crew. But how many vulnerable women are in this exact scenario? How many women are pressured to get into a car with a sketchy "professional" who's looking for cash and who knows what else?

Enough. It's time to step in. Watching this scene from my hiding place, and preparing myself for a confrontation with this shady locksmith, I feel the same thing I always do in these situations: *Calm.* It's strange. In most real-life situations, conflict makes me so nervous that my teeth chatter. I'm the guy who's too afraid to send back an overcooked steak at a restaurant. But when I'm about to confront someone on national television, with the risk of him taking a swing at me? Somehow I'm relaxed. I've prepared. I've done my homework. And I know I'm on the right side of the issue.

When you come face-to-face with this situation, you won't have a big TV crew and producers in your corner. So here's my advice for standing up for yourself without escalating the situation to conflict:

Challenge the locksmith or contractor (or whoever you think is ripping you off), by calmly saying things like, "Well I had another locksmith over here, and they told me something different." Or: "This happened to me once before, and the locksmith charged me half of what you're saying." Another: "That seems a little steep, I should get a second opinion." Most of them will start negotiating with you. Either way, you're subtly signaling that you're not about to get ripped off.

But since I do have a TV crew . . . let's do it this way. I come out of hiding and approach the locksmith. "Experts say you could have picked this lock in under a minute, and it's a hundred-dollar job. You charged her $685 and then demanded she pay you cash. You think that's right?"

"How can I help you, sir?" he says, busted.

"You can answer my questions. Are you a licensed locksmith?"

"Yes, I am," he says.

"Can I see your license?"

"No. You can't see anything."

"I'm just trying to figure out why you're trying to charge someone more than six times what experts say that job should cost."

"What do you want me to tell you?"

"What's your name?" I ask him.

"What's *my* name?" he snaps back, "What's *your* name?"

"Jeff Rossen of NBC News."

"Nice, nice name f$#k-face."

Somehow we avoid a fistfight, and happily, Ada does not have to get in a car with this guy. But in the end, *four out of the eight* locksmiths we called charged us too much, according to our expert . . . and mangled our locks in the process.

And there's more. We found some online locksmiths using fake addresses, making it nearly impossible to track them down if you want to lodge a complaint. Some are listed in parking lots, some track back to abandoned buildings, churches, and even schools.

There are a few things you can do to protect yourself. When you're in this situation, first *get the quote,* and get it in writing. Then, *before* they start working, tell them, "I don't have the cash on me, will you take a credit card?" This keeps things on the up and up.

And there are actually a couple of simple things you can do to keep yourself out of this scenario entirely. Leave a spare key at work or at a friend's house. Here's another: Before you have an emergency, when you have some free time on your hands, go into town and look for a legitimate locksmith—at an actual store in an actual building with actual employees. Get their card, program the number in your phone as "Locksmith," so if you're in a jam you won't get hustled by a guy who calls you "f$#k-face."

When the Bottom Falls Out . . . Literally

Your outdoor deck has a hidden danger. On the one hand, sure, what's not to love about it? You invite people over and barbecue on it, let the kids play on it. We never think twice about it. The deck looks safe.

But according to experts like Frank Libero of the American Society of Home Inspectors, a full 80 percent of decks have safety concerns. Sometimes this never causes a problem. But sometimes you see the tragedy of what happened in Indiana, where a group of teenagers posed for their prom picture on the deck and then, without warning, *BOOM!* the deck collapsed and came crashing down. Luckily those teenagers all survived, but scenes like this happen *every summer;* it's nearly a mathematical certainty.

Happily, there are a few easy ways to check and see if your deck is up to snuff. You're talking to the least handy guy, ever. Trust me, anyone can do this. *It will take less than five minutes* to inspect your deck, and look for a few very simple red flags:

RED FLAG 1: NAILS. "The very first thing you want to look at is where your deck attaches to the house," advises Ricardo Arevalo, a safety engineer with Simpson Strong-Tie. If the *only* method of attachment is nails, this is a signal of cheap, shoddy workmanship that could later cause a massive (and deadly) problem. A nail is smooth and pulls out very easily. They're great for hanging pictures on your wall, but not so great as your deck's foundational lynchpin. You need screws and bolts.

RED FLAG 2: ROTTING AND SPLINTERING WOOD. If the wood is rotted, it's far more likely to rip itself from the main house.

RED FLAG 3: A WOBBLY RAILING. Even if you tell your kids, "Don't lean against the railing!" it's human nature, and of course the kid will lean against the railing. So make sure it's sturdy.

RED FLAG 4: NAILS. Yep, it's so important that I'm listing it twice. Trust me: If all you see are nails, call a professional to inspect it.

Another bit of advice from the experts: Check your deck once a year. Here's a quick analogy: I'm fascinated by airplanes, so awhile back, I began taking classes to get a pilot's license. (Technically I went even further and got an "instrument rating," so I can fly in bad weather.) When I started training, the instructors told us to "treat every single flight like it's your first." In other words, I can't assume that because I haven't crashed in the last ten years, I'm not going to crash today. I have to remain vigilant. So with your deck, it's tempting to think that because it was sturdy five years ago and sturdy yesterday, it will be sturdy for the next five years. Wood rots. Metal rusts. So unless you're Bob Vila, it really is worth calling a professional home inspector.

Surviving Mother Nature

Whether you're in your home or traveling to someone else's, here's how to survive three of the most punishing acts of Mother Nature: earthquakes, tornadoes, and lightning.

EARTHQUAKES

South Africa. 2014. I was in my hotel room, flipping through channels on the TV, when I heard a weird sound from the corner of the room—*thunk*. My water bottle shook and rolled off the desk.

Thunk. A remote control started shaking and rolled off the desk, falling to the floor.

Thunk. Thunk. Thunk. More and more objects began crashing to the ground. *Thunk.* The walls started to shake. I grabbed onto my bed for dear life. I had no clue what to do. I knew that the expert advice somehow involved . . . a door. But is the advice to go under a door, or to *never* go to a door? Doors were either the best thing or the worst thing, I couldn't remember.

It was my first earthquake. And the experience haunts me, as it made me feel so ignorant, so powerless, so defenseless. What *should* you do in this situation? To find out, I traveled to the University of Nevada, Reno, where some very smart engineers have constructed an earthquake lab.

They built a simulated bedroom that sits on top of some "shakers," letting them rattle the walls and floors and sofas. "We can have earthquakes on demand," says Ian Buckle, the lab's director. *Great,* I think, *earthquakes on demand, just what I need.* He asks me to sit in the middle of the couch, and then he simulates a 6.9 quake.

Now, "6.9" doesn't sound that scary. It feels like a low number on the Richter scale. But even with a 6.9, man, things get scary *quick*. Cups fly off the table. The walls rattle. The bookshelf rocks back and forth, almost like a bucking bronco. Picture frames look ready to fly off the wall and smack me in the eye, and I have flashbacks to South Africa.

My key takeaway here: Even if the quake is not strong enough for your house to collapse around you, it still packs enough punch to turn your TV, your mantel, and even a remote control into deadly weapons. So if you live in an earthquake zone, experts advise securing heavy objects—like a computer printer, say—with earthquake-proofing tape that you can pick up for a few dollars.

And when the quake strikes, what do you do? "The rule of thumb is you duck, cover, and hold," says Buckle. (That means you crouch down, cover your head, and stay where you are.)

So what about hiding under the doorway? Many of us have always heard, "Hide under a door frame," but experts say that's not true. The door frame might not be sturdy at all. They say it's best to get under a table or a sturdy piece of furniture instead.

And if you're in a high-rise, maybe ten floors up? *Stay there.* Don't try to flee, as the stairs are likely even more dangerous.

"Stay on that floor," says Buckle, as you might get hit by flying debris. "Wait for the 'all clear.'"

Good to know.

TORNADOES

Tornadoes are random, and this is what makes them so scary. With a hurricane, by contrast, you have a little more warning and you could evacuate the entire town. But with a tornado? An entire house can be demolished, and then, across the street, not a single flower is touched. They're difficult to forecast. They're difficult to understand.

But to help you survive, I can quickly share what I learned from the best in the business, scientists at Texas Tech, who run a special lab that creates and simulates tornadoes, which gave me a taste of a tornado's awesome destruction.

At a warehouse in Lubbock, Texas, these mad scientists first simulate what's called an "EF0," with wind speeds of around 65 miles per hour. Their simulator sends planks of wood rocketing through the air and smashing through home siding. *Whoa.* And that's for the *weakest* kind of tornado. The strongest tornadoes, EF5s, have wind speeds of 250 miles per hour that can barrel toward your home.

Your first plan of attack: Grab couch cushions. As flimsy as that sounds, it gives you some protection in case wood or debris comes flying at you.

Your second move: Get to a bathtub, right? Now I'm a little less confident, but thankfully I have Rick Smith, with the National Weather Service, to set me straight.

"It depends on the house," says Smith. "There's nothing magically safe about a bathtub or a bathroom."

If the bathroom is near *any* outside wall of your home (front, back, or side), the bathtub might actually be the *last* place you want to hunker down. Why? "What you want to do is put as many walls between you and the tornado as you can," says Smith. Simply put, you want to be as close to the center of your home as possible. The more barriers between you and the storm outside, the better.

Smith walks me through a sample house, expertly taking in the floor plan, considering all the options. I ask him where we should hide.

"In this house it's a closet," he says.

"So once you get inside this closet what do you do?" I ask.

"We want to get down, get as low as we can possibly get, and we can cover up with these couch cushions," says Smith.

I enter the closet and pile the cushions on top of me, like a blanket. "So you put these cushions on top of you, literally like this?"

Smith explains that we need to shield ourselves from as much as possible. "Ride it out right here," he says.

I am now a grown man lying at the bottom of the closet, in the fetal position, holding cushions over my face as tightly as I can. I feel a bit ridiculous, but one thing I've learned is that in an emergency, you don't have time to worry about pride. Life—and tornadoes—are random like that.

LIGHTNING

I'll cut to the punch line: You really don't want to get struck by lightning—only a dummy would do that. (Luckily, I knew where to find one.) I wanted to know what it feels like for the hundreds of people who get struck by lightning every year. So I attended a disaster lab in Vancouver, Washington.

The evil geniuses in this lab strike dummies with terrifying bolts of electricity, and each one leaves a scar that would injure or kill you. Also? Lightning is LOUD. This surprised me. We think of lightning as a visual sign of terror, but when it strikes just twenty feet away, it sounds like a shotgun going off right next to your ear.

So how do you protect yourself?

At the first clap of thunder, you should seek shelter and stay inside. This next part is important: *Stay* inside for thirty minutes after you hear the last clap of thunder, even after you think it's safe—experts say that's enough time for you to know the storm has passed.

And as for trees? Think of them like doors in an earthquake—don't stand under them. That could increase your risk of being struck. Instead, move to the lowest elevation possible and *stay* low.

Before I leave the disaster lab, the experts give me one more sneaky tip. If you can't seek shelter, get inside a car. The reason? We've all heard that it's the rubber from the tires that grounds you, but that's actually not true. The *real* reason you're safer is because the electrical current stays on the outside (on the metal) and flows into the ground below.

So after the trips to these three labs, Mother Nature, I now say this to you: *Bring it.*

Kidding. Mother Nature, please stay far away. But if the worst-case scenario strikes, at least now you're ready.

Secret Spies Inside Your Bedroom

Your home is where you completely let your guard down. You're safe there. You have privacy.

But you know what you also have? A laptop or a computer of some kind. And nowadays, of course, almost every laptop comes with a front-facing camera, which we never really think about unless we're Skyping or FaceTiming.

Yet without any hints or warning, this camera can be hijacked by hackers, controlled remotely, who can watch you while you type, while you eat, while you sleep, while you come out of the shower, and even while you . . . yeah, that.

Just ask Cassidy Wolf, a young woman from California who, in 2013, was named Miss Teen USA. She was a target for the lowest of the low—a webcam predator who hacked into her laptop, spied on her, snapped intimate photos of her, and then blackmailed her. I couldn't say this on the air but I'll say it here: As a father (and as a human being) it makes me want to punch the guy in the face.

Cassidy agreed to open up and speak to me. "You would never think somebody would be watching you in your room," Cassidy told me. "It gave me nightmares."

"How did you find out about this?" I asked.

"I received an anonymous e-mail from an anonymous person,"

she said. "It basically was extorting me and blackmailing me. I saw that he had attached nude photos of me that he had taken in my bedroom."

You might think to yourself, *Well, I'm not a Miss Teen USA, so I'm not at risk.* False. The FBI investigated the case, and they found that this same webcam slimeball had also targeted a *dozen* other young women. Some were as young as sixteen years old.

Here's the even scarier truth: It's not that hard to hack. To get a sense of just how vulnerable *all* of us are, we set up an experiment with a family in suburban New Jersey. We first ask the father's permission, and then, with his blessing, we ask a security expert, Jim Stickley, to try to spy on the family remotely. Stickley never lays a finger on their laptops. He practices his dark arts from the comfort of his own swivel chair, clacking away on his keyboard, thousands of miles away.

"People who are victims generally have no idea that they are victims," says Stickley. Then he shows me an e-mail that he sent to the New Jersey family, a harmless-looking e-card that has a little cartoon that looks like Donald Duck. When they opened that card, all they saw was the duck quacking. But behind the scenes, Stickley had unleashed a Trojan virus that wormed its way through their computer, giving him full access to the webcam. The family had no clue.

Like something out of a sci-fi movie, on Stickley's monitor he could now view the family laughing and eating dinner. And all it took was a few simple lines of code. Hackers can also slither into the cameras on your smartphone and your tablet.

Okay, enough. I don't want to invade this family's privacy longer than a few minutes—I got the idea—so we stop recording and a couple days later I visit the house, ring the doorbell, officially introduce myself, and sit down with them in their living room.

"Anyone ever hack into your system at home?" I ask the parents and the girls.

"I don't think so, no," says one of the girls.

Time to drop the bombshell. "We actually recorded your family dinner the other night," I say, and I know how creepy that must sound. (Remember, we had the father's permission. But still.) "No one was in your house except for you guys."

"It's really creepy," the mother says. "I mean—my children are on their computers in the evening in their bedrooms."

This is true. And our hacker knew it. We still have access to the webcam, and I show the mom a live video of the girls in their bedroom upstairs. I instantly recognize the look of panic on her face—as a parent I know the look well. (Don't worry, we had our own female producer in the room as well, to ensure they wouldn't do anything they wouldn't also do in public.)

"I . . . I'm sick over it," says the mom. "I really am. It's very upsetting."

I know this is tough on the mom, and I begin to feel bad about the whole icky operation, but then she looks at me. "I actually appreciate it," she says. "Because I'm hoping I can learn from this and try to avoid this ever happening."

That's the goal here. Some of these experiments can be awkward or unsettling, but they all have a mission of raising a larger awareness, and to help *all of us* be more safe. The FBI says that webcam hacking is a growing issue, and more and more people are being spied on . . . even when they don't know it.

So, a few takeaways. Think carefully about clicking any links in e-mails. If they're from someone you don't know, and especially if they show a quacking duck, do *not* open the attachment. And when you're not using your laptop, *close* the damn thing. That camera can work even during sleep mode. The safest thing you can do is stick a black piece of tape over the camera itself. Doesn't sound very hi-tech, but even the FBI director says he does that on his own laptop. Yeah, the *head of the FBI* does it, so now I do it, too. And it's not coming off any time soon.

By the way, the FBI eventually caught the predator who blackmailed Miss Teen USA. Was it some lecherous old hacker who had spent years honing his craft? Maybe a black-ops, ex-military specialist? A foreign terrorist? Nope. Just a teenager who had been one of her high school classmates. Hackers can come from anywhere. So stay smart.

2

TRAVEL DANGERS REVEALED

W E NEVER REALLY THINK ABOUT it, but every day we dodge a flurry of missiles and landmines and projectiles—on the road. Cars can kill us, frustrate us, and nearly bankrupt us. Same with planes and trains.

- How to Survive a Raging Flood
- How to Survive a Plane Crash
- Driving While Drowsy
- Screwing You Under the Hood
- Germs on a Plane
- What Are Your Rights When Police Pull You Over?
- How to Survive a Train Crash
- Look Out! Beware of Flying Mattresses
- How to Survive an Ice Skid

How to Survive a Raging Flood

My phone vibrates. It's a text from my wife, Danielle: "You're crazy."

She's not wrong. The night before, I told her that I would simulate getting stuck inside a car that's being flooded with freezing water—like Harry Houdini but without a lock pick. (Confession: I used to tell my wife about these things two weeks before the experiment, and I've found that when I tell her that far in advance, she has the ability to talk me out of it. But if I tell her the night before? It's too late to back out, and the train has already left the station. What can I say, you didn't buy this book for marriage advice. . . .)

The reason for this experiment is simple: Flash floods are everywhere, they are sudden, they are scary, and they are deadly. The worst part? They can be far more dangerous than they appear. The raging *Perfect Storm*–looking waves are the images that you see on the news, but often it's the calm, shallow floods that put you the most at risk. You might think, *Hey, I've got an SUV, I'm good to go,* but this might lull you into a false sense of security. You'd be surprised at how little water it takes to float a car or flip a car, even an SUV. And what happens if you get stuck? How do you get out?

This is where my experiment kicks in. Because my wife is right and I do crazy things, I travel to a flood-training course in Whistler, Canada, where they use their outdoor laboratory—there's a laboratory for everything—to create a raging flood.

"Even a foot of water could make a car float," says Jim Douglas, a certified trainer with Raven Rescue. He adds that if you're in an SUV or a 4x4, ironically, you might be even *more* at risk, "Those big tires will make a truck float even easier. They're like big buoys."

Okay. Go time. I'm sitting in a pickup truck, which, thankfully, has been chained to the ground so it doesn't float away (I don't have a death wish.) The water comes straight at me . . . now I know there's no turning back. Up until then it had all been abstract—now it's real. The water seeps in through the bottom of the car, like a boat that's getting flooded, and soon the water touches a piece of skin that's between my jeans and my moccasins. It's cold and icy, a lick of the frozen tundra.

They had warned me that the water was going to be cold, but nothing prepared me for the subarctic freeze.

The cold makes a difference. Because your body is physically in pain, you're not only dealing with the mental stress of how you'll escape from the situation, you're also dealing with a shutdown of your body. The jeans stick to me, and it's a terrifying and disgusting feeling. To give some perspective: Jump in your pool in the dead of winter and you'll get maybe one-fiftieth of the sensation. Not to mention you're freaking out because your car is floating away.

"You need to roll the window down!" Douglas yells from where he's standing nearby, yanking me from my panic. *Right.* I had forgotten. When you're seized by panic it's difficult to function normally. Douglas gives some surprising advice: "Rolling down the window" when you're getting flooded might sound as logical as, say, lighting a match when you're in a burning home, but this is a critical tip that most people don't understand.

\ \ \ | / / /

The second the water rises, roll down the window.

/ / / | \ \ \

When the water hits your door, the pressure is too great. The Hulk himself couldn't push it open. So you know I can't. And you can't either. Since the door is stuck, the window is your only way out of the vehicle. So I roll down the window and climb out. (Note: Climbing out a window is awkward, but doable).

"Get on the roof of the truck!" yells Douglas over the roaring flood.

The water is blasting at me, pelting my face, freezing me, and nearly paralyzing me.

"Get on the roof of the truck!" Douglas yells again.

The water keeps pouring in as I struggle to escape—did I mention it is cold?—and I try to slither out of the window. Trust me, this is not as easy as they make it look on *The Dukes of Hazzard*. I get out just in the nick of time. In just seconds the water has risen all the way past the gas pedal, past the seat, past the top of the steering wheel, and approaches the roof of the car. If I had been just a little bit slower climbing out of that window, I would have been a goner and my wife would have had the last laugh.

Now I'm on the roof, but I have a new set of problems: *Now, what?*

"Now . . . get stable, stay low!" barks out Douglas. "Hang on. With the truck moving you're going to have to ride with it." You need to look for a tree—a branch—anything to grab on to. Otherwise, stay on that roof.

Oh God. If this were a real flood without the safety chain, I would now be surfing on the roof of a truck that is literally sailing out of control. Even *with* the chain it's scary as hell and it's difficult to keep your balance. The water sprays at my face and makes it difficult to see or to think. The advice from the experts: *Stay as low as you can and hang on for dear life.*

But the real advice here? Don't go anywhere near these floods. Seriously. If you see even the shallowest of floods on the street, turn around and find another route. Even if you're late for your job or your dinner or your doctor's appointment. I learned that a car can float (or flip) in very shallow water, it can float in six feet of water, and it can float anywhere in between. If you're trapped inside you can easily get killed. If you make it to the roof you have a better chance.

Just avoid the situation. In fact, in Arizona, this is such a problem that the state has created something called the "Stupid Motorist Law." Too many Arizona drivers—either macho or oblivious—had decided to plow their SUVs through the water and forge ahead. Some died, some lived, and most of them risked the lives of the rescuers, too. Thanks to the "Stupid Motorist Law" in Arizona, if you've been rescued after driving in the flood waters, you may have to pay for the entire rescue operation yourself.

So maybe my wife is right and maybe I'm crazy but, thanks to this lesson, hopefully a few more people, at least, will be a little less stupid.

How to Survive a Plane Crash

I fly all the time, and I'll admit that I fly so much, I sort of zone out when the flight attendant is giving the instructions. While they're giving a safety speech that is designed to SAVE MY LIFE, I secretly stare at my phone and check e-mail or Twitter. *I know what to do in case of emergency*, I tell myself. How hard can it be? So many times over the years—dozens, hundreds—I sat in the exit row, and the flight attendant would ask me, "Can you open the door yada yada yada in case of emergency?" I would smile, say yes, and go back to checking my e-mail.

Apparently I was doing it all wrong.

Most of us are.

This is especially strange when you consider that plane crashes are traumatic, chaotic, and violent. They're both horrific and fascinating. I'll confess that I watch YouTube videos of plane crashes (that's not normal?). Think about the passengers in a crash. Just minutes earlier they're reading or sleeping, and then . . . the engines go silent. The lights might darken. It's eerie. It's confusing.

So to find out what we should *really* do in a crash, my team was given rare access to Delta's flight attendant training facility, one of the most intense programs in the country. They put me on an airplane and then simulate a crash. There's smoke, mock fire, and shaking. I'm disoriented. I jump from my chair and make a beeline for the closest exit, the front door, and then prepare to open it.

Wrong.

A flight attendant blocks me from that door. Wait, what did I do wrong?

"She blocked you because she saw fire outside," explains Liz Layton, a veteran flight attendant with more than eighteen years of experience. "That's why there's a flight attendant at each exit. We encourage passengers to never, ever open up our exits."

I'm a little confused. "So passengers should never open a door?"

"Never."

Wait. But now I'm lost. "I fly a lot, and sometimes I end up sitting in the exit row," I explain, "and the flight attendant always comes by and says, 'Are you willing and able to open the door?' So what's that about?" I thought I'm supposed to open the door and be the hero.

"Are you willing and able to *assist* us, if we need you in an emergency?" Layton clarifies. "You must follow our instructions."

"So don't open this door by myself unless you tell me to?"

"Exactly."

How many millions of Americans are just as confused as me?

Back to the simulation—as I scramble to leave my seat, I quickly pause to grab my phone.

Wrong.

"Leave everything," Layton patiently explains. "Including purses and phones. Leave everything."

It's true. If you get in a plane crash, you might just have to go a few hours without checking Twitter or Facebook. No one said survival was easy.

Once I leave my seat and hustle out of the (correct) exit, I jump down the inflatable slide, feet first, with my arms folded across my chest, sort of like you do on a waterslide.

Wrong.

"You need to put your arms straight ahead when you go down the slide," says Layton.

I try and visualize this in my head: arms out in front of you, and then you go feetfirst down the slide. "Sort of like you're a zombie?" I ask.

"Yes!"

There's a logic behind this: If you jump down the slide with your arms extended, it will be easier for the folks at the bottom to pull you up, and this prevents a logjam at the end of the slide. (I'll confess, though, that I never did manage to get the jump right. Sorry Liz. Next time . . .)

We also simulate what you should do if the plane crashes into water. You know how you have the inflatable life vest under your seat? You might think that it's important to grab the vest, open it, put it over your head, and then inflate the sucker as soon as possible.

Wrong.

"It's very important *not* to inflate your life vest while you're inside the airplane," instructs Layton. "You're going to wait for the flight attendants to call you to the door." If you inflate your vest inside the plane and the cabin fills with water, then you're pinned against the ceiling and can't escape. While inside the plane, you want the ability to swim underwater to the exit.

Once at the door of the plane, and staring into a pool of water, she finally tells me to inflate the vest. So I yank the red tabs, pull it hard, and then it quickly inflates.

"Jump into the water!" yells Liz. "Swim to that raft! Swim!"

I jump into the water and kick my legs, trying to swim. When is the last time you swam while fully clothed? It is *hard*. The clothes make you slow and sluggish, and just think about how much harder it would be if you were paddling away from a burning 747 about to explode.

I make it to the raft and clamber on board, surviving the "crash" and, more importantly, learning that I've been doing most things wrong for so many years. Yet here's some good news: According to the National Transportation Safety Board, most airplane crashes *are* survivable. The key is to actually listen to your flight attendants . . . and maybe check your e-mail another time.

Driving While Drowsy

We, as a civilization, are afraid to utter two very simple words: *I'm tired*. We have a fear of looking weak. If we confess that we're tired, it somehow feels like we're admitting defeat, a loser, or not a good enough mom or dad or man or woman. I'm guilty of this. When I get a call from NBC at 3 A.M. because of breaking news, sometimes they'll say, "Did I wake you?" and for whatever reason I lie and say, "No, you didn't." Why are we so afraid of admitting we're sleepy?

Even when we're exhausted, we rarely think twice about getting behind the wheel. We know it's wrong to drive drunk, but we feel it's less of a taboo to drive while drowsy. This costs lives. Drowsy driving causes more than 100,000 crashes a year, according to the National Sleep Foundation, along with an estimated 71,000 injuries and 1,550 deaths.

But statistics are one thing, and my gut tells me something different. Sure, *those* people nodded off at the wheel and crashed their cars, but I'm better than that. I'm a good driver. I have iron willpower.

So the idea of a "drowsy driving experiment" seemed like a piece of cake. After surviving floods and simulated airplane crashes, how hard can this be? I head to a technical obstacle course at the Skip Barber Racing School in Lakeville, Connecticut, where I would navigate their course two different times: once while wide awake, and once after nearly thirty hours without sleep.

The first time through the course, I deftly swerve between the orange cones, make some nifty lane changes, and take the sharp turns with no problem. It's not exactly a NASCAR debut, but I ace it.

Then I keep myself awake for nearly thirty hours. At 2 A.M. I watch some bad TV, at 3 A.M. I zombie-watch some infomercials, and at 4 A.M. I go out for some critical nutrients (a slice of pizza). The next morning I feel a little groggy, but when I arrive at the course my adrenaline kicks in, I rally, and I know that I'm ready for action. I've driven sleepier than this before. Most people have.

I turn the keys, ease the car forward, and worry that this is maybe a wasted "experiment," as the results are pretty ho-hum— I feel okay. I can operate the vehicle just fine. I wonder if we should cancel the project. *Clunk.* I just ran over an orange cone.

I swerve into the next lane—*clunk, clunk, clunk*—and trample more cones. *Where did those bastards come from?* My reflexes are slow, my nerves frayed. After smashing through a few more cones, mercifully, the course sends me to a nice, straight, empty road where I can just drive in peace. No sudden lane changes, no traffic, no obstacles, no cones. I begin to relax and ease into a nice driving rhythm.

BOOM!

I crash into a line of cones that had been placed on the street, appearing out of nowhere. I didn't see them until too late . . . even though they were bright orange and clearly visible. I must have nodded off. If that had been a car—or a person—someone would be dead.

I had experienced what experts call "micro-sleep," that tiny sliver of sleep that can lead to fatal accidents. "Most people don't realize that part of the brain can be asleep while another part of the brain is awake," says Dr. Charles Czeisler, a sleep expert from Boston's Brigham and Women's Hospital. "So you may be able to keep your foot full throttle on the accelerator, and yet not have the judgment area of the brain engaged."

In fact, experts say that when you feel that moment of nodding off—and entering micro-sleep—that's an excellent predictor that you *will* actually nod off. Our mind plays tricks. When we nod off we think that we get a "jolt" of adrenaline and suddenly we're wide awake but, in reality, it's the opposite. If you nod off once, you will almost certainly nod off twice. This is part of why losing sleep for one night is the equivalent of being legally drunk. And that's, well, eye-opening.

So, late one night, while driving home from my daughter's sleep-away camp, I had a five-hour drive ahead of me and I felt myself nodding off. The "manly" thing would've been to fight through the fatigue. Instead I pulled over, stopped the car, and turned to my wife. "Do you mind taking the wheel?"

Danielle smiled and we swapped places. I leaned back in the seat and the car moved forward in the darkness. It felt good—and honest—to admit those two little words: *I'm tired.*

Screwing You Under the Hood

There are two kinds of people in the world: those who get a flat tire and can fix it themselves, and the people like me, who need to call AAA. I know nothing about cars. I don't know a carburetor from a muffler, an alternator from a distributor.

Here's what I do know: When the little blinking light comes on that says there's a problem, I need to bring it to a mechanic.

Yet these experts, of course, *know* that I'm clueless. They can smell it. When I walk into a car shop, as soon as I open my mouth, they can tell that I wouldn't be able to change a spark plug. (The spark plug is in the trunk, right?) And my ignorance is exploited. In one of my favorite *Seinfeld* episodes, Puddy works at the auto dealership, and he and Elaine, like always, are breaking up. He tacks on a bunch of add-ons to Jerry's bill, including "rust-proofing," "transport charge," "storage surcharge," and "additional overcharge."

When they get back together (like always), he laughs and cuts Jerry a break, saying of the charges, "Oh, we don't even know what it is!"

So we all have that gnawing fear that repairmen are ripping us off. Are we being paranoid, or is that actually happening?

Time for an undercover experiment.

Exhibit A: Our four-year-old SUV. It's under 40,000 miles and out of warranty. We first take it to a mechanic who's certified by two top auto repair groups. He has a goatee, a shaved head, and tattoos up and down each forearm. He inspects every system of our SUV and gives it a clean score.

"Everything looks fine. Everything is good," the mechanic says with satisfaction.

Then we ask him to rig a very simple problem . . . something that any mechanic worth his salt could spot in a second. So he takes a tiny part from the air conditioner, the "relay switch" (beats me) that's about the size of a plastic LEGO block and he swaps it for a defective one.

"And that makes the air-conditioning blow warm air?" I ask.

"Yes."

"Quick and easy fix?"

"Yeah. Just replace the relay and that's it."

This guy, our trusty mechanic, says he'd charge only $100 to fix it. What would the auto-repair chains charge? We send our fearless producer, Kelly, undercover to pose as a hapless car owner.

Her first stop is a big-name chain with locations all over the country. Within minutes the mechanic pops the hood, pokes around, and correctly diagnoses our bad relay as the only problem.

"So it's pretty simple?" asks Kelly.

"Uh-huh."

And pretty cheap. They only charge ninety-one bucks—a little *less* than our independent mechanic suggested. Not bad. Kelly gets the same result at another company in New Jersey—only ninety. At the third stop, a different chain, the manager goes one step further, saying that Kelly doesn't even need him, that she could buy the relay switch herself at an auto-parts store for just twenty-five bucks, and easily replace it.

But then Kelly's luck takes a darker turn. At one repair shop, the mechanic quickly spots the bad relay, but then says that fixing her A/C requires some extra services and an "A/C recharge package." (Did he get that from Puddy?) *And* a brand-new air filter. Total charge? $464 . . . or almost *five times* what it should actually cost.

"Your cabin air filter is very dirty," the mechanic tells Kelly with a straight face.

Except it isn't. We know this because our original mechanic inspected the filter, giving it a clean bill of health. In fact, just to be extra careful, our tattooed mechanic checked our A/C pressure before every stop—and each time it was fine.

Since *I* am clearly not a car authority, we consulted with expert Paul DeGuiseppi, one of the nation's top A/C repair mechanics, and Phil Reed, senior editor of a popular auto website.

"What he's doing right there is using the little bit of knowledge he has to try to convince you [that] you need some things you don't need," says DeGuiseppi.

The experts say that the A/C, in particular, is a dicey area that's prone to overcharges. "This is probably the easiest go-to place for them to make money," says Reed. "Over the . . . lifetime of a car, it adds up to really thousands of dollars."

Things get even worse at our next stop. For some reason the mechanic *never even checks the relay*—the only problem with our SUV—and instead comes back to Kelly with a more serious problem (that we know isn't really a problem at all).

"This valve is leaking," the mechanic says. "This shit's been leaking for a while."

It gets worse.

"We have to replace this part, and then recharge the system again," the mechanic says.

The total is $393. . . . to fix a problem that never existed.

DeGuiseppi, the A/C expert, is clearly saddened by the overcharging. "It's people like this that give us all a bad name," he says. "There really are a lot of good people out there."

"They're abusing our trust," says Reed. "Because, in many cases, they appeal to us as the trusted adviser, and yet they're actually picking our pockets."

If you think you'll have better luck at the official dealerships—maybe, maybe not. We took the same SUV—with the same defective relay—to several authorized dealerships. Again Kelly went undercover. Again there was nothing wrong with our SUV other than the relay switch.

One mechanic properly identified the defective relay, but also wanted to give our A/C a system recharge: $150.

One found a problem with the transmission: $229.

The brake flush: $159.

Fuel induction and emissions services: $339.

When the dust settled, one dealership wanted to charge poor Kelly $2,171 for a bundle of services . . . none of which, according to our independent mechanic, was actually needed.

There are three things you can do to protect yourself:

1) Actually read the owner's manual—this can help demystify some of the mechanic's mumbo jumbo, giving you a clearer sense of what the car actually needs. For example (bonus tip!), if your manual says your car takes 87 octane, spending more on 89 isn't worth it.

2) Ask friends for recommendations before your car breaks down. It's like dating. Word of mouth and a personal connection is always safer.

3) Once your car does break down and you get that first price, get a second opinion. Because, for every honest tattooed mechanic, you might run into a Puddy.

Germs on a Plane

Flight delays. Long lines at security. Overpriced food. Crying babies. These are all the things you know and love about the airport, but they might pale compared to something invisible, something sneaky, and something that none of us really cares to think about: hidden germs.

I take this stuff seriously, as the airport is my home away from home. So I was a bit terrified when we decided to investigate the airports and airplanes for hidden germs. If they're oozing with invisible slime, would I need to walk around in a rubber bodysuit? (Great for avoiding germs, not so great for my marriage.)

To investigate, the Rossen Reports team crisscrossed the country on three different flights, testing for germs at every step of the journey: the check-in kiosks, the TSA bins, the seats' armrests, the tray tables—the works.

Our first stop is the check-in kiosk. Every day, thousands of people wipe their grubby little hands all over that screen. We gently rub the screen with a cotton swab that looks like a Q-tip. After we send the sample to a certified laboratory to be analyzed by microbiologists, it comes back . . . clean! Thank you, America, for washing your hands. Off to a strong start.

Next comes the security line, also known as the land of smelly feet. Think about those bins. "Empty everything out of your pockets," the agents tell us, and that *usually* means car keys and phones and wallets. But who knows what people carry around in their pockets?

We get to the stack of TSA bins. My producer Jovanna's white Q-tip immediately gets dirty, and, in fact, it looks something like . . . brown. . . . *Ew.*

The test results confirm our darkest fears: The TSA bin had fecal matter on it.

"That's disgusting!" one woman exclaims, echoing all our thoughts.

The scientists use fancier language, but they basically agree. "We're talking about skin or soft-tissue infections," says Dr. Robert Glatter, who works the emergency room at New York's Lenox Hill Hospital, after analyzing our results. "Which can potentially lead to overwhelming infections in your bloodstream."

So it's not just gross—it's potentially dangerous.

And on that happy note, time to board our flight! It doesn't take advanced sensors for us to note the visible crumbs in the carpet, or a brown smudge on a seat that looks like—best-case scenario—smeared chocolate from a Snickers bar. Delicious.

To find out how dirty things can truly get, we talk to a veteran flight attendant, Hollis Gillespie.

"It disgusts me, but it doesn't really surprise me," says Hollis. She says that the tray tables are used for much, *much* more than what you would expect. Like, for example, "changing the baby's diaper."

"Where we eat?" I ask, feeling sick.

"Yes."

So my team swabs the tray tables, arm rests, and seat belts. The tray tables—you know, that place where you wipe your baby's bottom—have the highest levels of bacteria. The armrests come back clean. But the seat belts? Filthy. In fact, they have something that the experts call "human bacteroides."

"That sounds serious," I say to Dr. Glatter.

"It's very serious," says Dr. Glatter, who wears a white lab coat and looks very serious indeed. "These are bacteria that live in our gut and our intestines. These are dangerous bacteria that cause serious infections."

"All from touching one of those surfaces?"

"Absolutely."

In total we took thirteen samples. Nine of them came back positive for germs. So what's the root cause of the problem? Most airlines say that they wipe down every surface, every table, and every armrest between each flight. But insiders say that's impossible. Even though they work their tails off, the ground crews just don't have time. They can't keep up. How could they?

And hey, I'm guilty, too. On my last flight, I took a half-eaten sea-salted caramel and stuck it in the seat pocket in front of me. (AMER-ICA, I HAVE SINNED.) I told myself, *The ground crew will get it.* But will they? This tiny kind of infraction happens all the time, and they add up.

"What can the airlines do to make these planes cleaner?" I ask Hollis Gillespie, the veteran flight attendant.

"They could schedule longer turnaround times between flights. And it would be a more sanitary environment for their passengers," she says. Yet that, of course, would mean fewer flights each day, and that would mean less revenue. (I'm not betting on it.)

But here's what we can do to trim the risk of infection: Never walk around barefoot (even on long international flights), bring plenty of wipes, use gobs of hand sanitizer, inspect the pocket on the seat in front of you, and avoid sitting next to guys who chew sea-salted caramels. And, if all else fails, rock the rubber bodysuit.

What Are Your Rights When Police Pull You Over?

It feels like every month, every week, and almost every day there's a new awful story. A "routine" traffic stop that turns deadly. These stories are tragic. They're heartbreaking.

I don't pretend to have any pat solutions to the complex issues of criminal justice or race relations. But when it comes to the traffic stops themselves, part of the problem is something very basic and very human: *Confusion.* We're just not sure how to act. We're not sure about our rights. Do I have to let the cop search my car? Am I allowed to film the scene with my phone? Do I need to say *Yes* to everything? Could this stuff be used against me in court?

In fact, just two weeks before writing this, I was pulled over for illegally crossing into an HOV carpool lane. When the police officer walked up and rapped her knuckles on the window, all kinds of worst-case scenarios tumbled through my mind. I had nothing to hide and I knew it was only a minor infraction, but it *still* makes you nervous. And it's worth remembering that the cop is anxious, too. I'm not a killer . . . but she doesn't know that.

So to get a clearer understanding of your rights as a driver, I allow myself to get "pulled over" by the police department in Rochester, New York. Lieutenant Henry Favor, an exceedingly polite, friendly man, is kind enough to do a bit of role-playing.

Sitting in the driver's seat, in my rearview mirror I watch as Lieutenant Favor walks up to my car. I keep my hands on the steering wheel, at ten and two. I roll down the window and he explains how it works.

"The very first thing I would ask for is license, registration, and proof of insurance," says Lieutenant Favor.

"And I have to give you this?"

"Yes, sir. That's one thing you're required to give me. The next thing I might ask you is, 'Do you know why I stopped you?'"

This question has always thrown me for a loop. It seems like it might be a way of getting trapped, or even confessing. "Let's say I know that I was speeding," I say. "I know I did something wrong. I don't want to admit guilt to you. Do I have to answer that question?"

"You don't have to answer that question," says Lieutenant Favor. *Interesting.* How many people get this part wrong? "You can say a couple of things," he suggests. "You can say 'I don't know,' 'no,' or not say anything at all."

"And I'm not more likely to get a ticket because of that?"

"No, sir."

"What if I want to record this interaction to protect myself?" I ask him, holding up my camera-phone. "There's been a lot of controversy about people recording police. Am I allowed to record this?"

Lieutenant Favor doesn't miss a beat. "You are allowed to record. I may even have a body camera on myself, or my car may be equipped with one. You're absolutely allowed to record."

But before I reach for my phone . . .

"Couple things you've got to be careful of, though," Lieutenant Favor quickly adds. "The first thing is not to make any sudden movements in the vehicle, or reach in areas that we can't see. Last thing I want to do is think [the phone] is a weapon."

Got it. "So what I want to do is say, 'Officer, I want to record this. I'm taking my phone out, I'm pointing it at you, and I am recording.'" I pick up my phone and point the camera at Lieutenant Favor, with him standing just inches away, outside the driver's window. It would take some serious chutzpah to record a conversation like this. My guess is that most people don't realize that it's legal, and many people would be too threatened to actually keep the video rolling. "And this is fine?" I ask, amazed.

"And that is fine," he says.

Sometimes the traffic stop might end right there—maybe with a ticket or a warning. Sometimes, of course, things take a different turn.

"The next thing that may happen, I may have reason to ask you to step out of the car," says Lieutenant Favor.

I feel like I'm on a roll with these newfound rights that I didn't realize I had, so I ask him, "What if I say I *don't want* to get out of the car?"

He shakes his head. "This is another one of those things that you *have* to do."

Fair enough. If the cop asks you to get out of the car, you need to do it. No wiggle room. Fighting will only make things worse. He asks me again to get out of the car—politely, as always—and I slowly open the door and step out. But I know myself, and I know that if I were in this situation for real, I'd be confused and indignant and I might ask him something like *This is a routine traffic stop, why am I out of the car? What's the problem?*

"I may tell you or I may not," Lieutenant Favor says.

"You don't have to?"

"I do not have to. No, sir."

Ah, so two can play at the game of "selective sharing." You don't have to voluntarily share any wrongdoing, and the officer doesn't have to explain why you're being removed from your car.

"Another thing I may ask is, 'You don't mind if I search your car, do you?'" says Lieutenant Favor.

"Well, I don't think anyone wants their car searched. Do I have to say yes to that?"

"You don't. It's a request. I'm asking for consent," says the Lieutenant. Even though it sounds like a command, it's really just a question.

I think about how sometimes cops say things like *Come on buddy, what are you trying to hide? Why don't you let me search you?* Lieutenant Favor admits, "That's a tactic that we use trying to elicit conversation. . . ." In other words, basically, it's a type of trap.

"I shouldn't feel bullied to say yes?" I ask.

"Nope. It's still a request."

"And can it hurt me in court if I say no?"

"No, it cannot."

\ \ \ \ | / / /,

THE BOTTOM LINE: In the chaos and confusion of a traffic stop, believe it or not, there are only two things that you have to do, according to Lieutenant Favor. "You have to provide your license, registration, and proof of insurance. And then you have to get out of the car when we tell you to." And that's it. Other things might *sound* like commands, but they're often just cleverly worded questions.

/ / / | | \ \ \ \

Of course, laws can vary from state to state and city to city but, wherever you are, remember to be polite to the officer—even if you're frustrated and angry. And if they *do* search your car against your will without probable cause, don't fight with him on the scene. You're better off fighting it in court.

I can't predict the future, but one thing I'm sure of is that sometime in life, for right or wrong, I'll again be pulled over by the police. Now I'll know how to handle myself.

How to Survive a Train Crash

When we're teenagers and we learn how to drive, we get a multi-week driver's ed course. When we get in a plane, we get a safety message from the flight attendants. Even when we get on a boat, there's usually some sort of safety briefing.

Yet when we get on a train? Nothing. There's no video, no brochure, no friendly speech about the "nearest exit." You're pretty much on your own.

Most of the time, of course, we're happy with this arrangement.

Trains are usually safe. Convenient. It's nice to just hop on and hop off, no muss, no fuss. But there are *thousands* of train accidents every year and, in a lot of these cases, the passengers have no idea how to escape. How could they? No one ever told them how.

This isn't just some theoretical "what if." In 2015, a Metro-North commuter train in New York slammed into an SUV and burst into flames, sending all of the passengers into a panic. Some struggled to escape, confused. Six people died.

So after that tragedy, I decided to do a little digging.

First off, where is the safest place to sit in the train?

"You want to be in the middle of the train," says Paul Worley, from the North Carolina Department of Transportation. "It's the least likely car, or set of cars, to derail." You don't want to be in the front or the back, because if there's a crash, that's where the energy is.

Bonus tip: Sit facing backward. This way if there's a crash, you'll be pushed back in your seat, instead of thrown forward.

Okay, but in the worst-case scenario and your train does crash, *how do you escape?*

I consult with Scott Sauer, a safety expert for SEPTA, Philadelphia's regional rail service. I join him on an actual train and we walk down the empty rows of seats, looking at the doors and the windows and the possible avenues of escape. Scott has a trim goatee and short, military-cropped hair.

"The first and the best way, is to go car to car," says Scott. "If you have a problem in the car that you're sitting in, go to the next car."

This might sound obvious, but people forget this when they're stuck in the smoky chaos of a crash—they think only about *their* car, when there might be safer options just a few cars away.

"If that doesn't work, what do you do next?"

"Every train in the country has emergency signs," says Scott, pointing to one that I hadn't really noticed. It's funny how our brain blocks out these emergency-exit signs—they just blend into the background, like the quiet humming of our refrigerator. "If you see the sign, you can even open the main door. . . ." He points to some instructions printed on the wall; I hadn't noticed those, either.

"So even if the conductor or the engineer are too busy . . . to open the door, you can open it yourself?" I ask.

"Absolutely."

Let's do this. Following the easy-to-read instructions, I lift a little ring on a panel of the wall. The panel swings open. Inside is a red handle, and I push it down. The train door opens. The entire operation took less than three seconds, but most people have no idea that the panel even exists.

When the door opens I stare down at the ground, several feet below me, surprised that we're so high up. (But that makes sense. Normally when you leave a train, you just step onto the platform, which is at the same elevated level.) So I carefully climb down off the train, and then, when my feet land on the gravel, I follow another bit of Scott's advice: *Look both ways.*

Most people forget this. If you're escaping from a train in a panic, the instinct is to jump from the car and sprint far away. But guess what's next to most train tracks? *More* train tracks. Running from a crashed train and then getting splattered by *another* train, well, is something of a rookie mistake.

And be careful not to get electrocuted. In the case of Metro-North and in many spots across the country, there's an electrified third rail that can kill you instantly. Stay on your toes.

I hop back on the train and grill Scott again. What happens if the door is somehow impaired?

"In every train car there are emergency-exit windows," says Scott, pointing to the glass. He grabs a red handle and gives it a tug. "You're gonna take the handle, you're gonna pull it." The red rubber lining from the window easily peels away. Then he grabs the window's handle. "Pull the window toward you. And then you can get out of the window, but remember it's still a seven- to eight-foot drop to the ground. So you have to be aware of that."

Yet there's one final scenario I need to play out. In the Metro-North crash there was an explosion, a fire, and then puffs of smoke that nearly blinded the passengers. It was confusing and terrifying and deadly. How do you prepare for *that?*

Scott shows me. He fills the train with simulated smoke, and a gray haze swirls through the car. I can barely see. It looks like a train on fire, or maybe an eighties-era heavy metal video. Without any guidance, I'd almost certainly freak out.

The secret? Look *down*. Odds are you never noticed this, but the walkways in trains are lined with streaks of yellow. This is more than a fashion statement—it's a glow-in-the-dark trail. "You want to get on the floor," says Scott, dropping to his hands and knees, and then crawling through the aisle. I follow him. "Follow the striping on the floor . . . it's gonna take you where you need to go. You want to get to . . . the end of the car, where your exit is."

When the smoke clears I thank him. "And if you commit these to memory, it's the best way to stay safe?"

"That's right."

Later, after I share these tips, the *Today* show cohost Savannah Guthrie sums it up perfectly. "We hope it never happens, but it's good to be prepared." Words to live by.

Look Out! Beware of Flying Mattresses

Midnight. Los Angeles. I'm on the I-405, driving from the airport to my hotel, grateful for the lack of traffic. I'm cruising at around sixty miles per hour. All of a sudden, my headlights catch a flicker of something on the ground. Before my mind can process this . . .

Boom!

I see splintered wood flying past the windshield. The car shakes violently. I can hear the sound of glass crunching from underneath the car. *Crunch, crunch, crunch.* I swerve into the next lane—thank God no one was there. My heart is pounding.

In the rearview mirror, now I can see what happened: I had just run over a bookshelf. It was the kind of massive, wood-and-glass bookshelf that your grandma might have owned; the way they used to make 'em, heavy and big. It must have fallen off a trailer and someone had just left it there, abandoned, like a booby trap. The entire left side of my car is caved in. It could have killed me. It could have killed you.

This could be anything: a bookcase, a mattress, plywood, or a Christmas tree. It turns out this happens *all the time.* Flying debris kills nearly 500 people every year and injures 11,000 more, according to the National Highway Traffic Safety Administration, and the root cause is very simple: People don't know how to tie this stuff down.

Let's focus on a common example: mattresses. I reach out to

Trooper Steven Michael, of the Washington State Patrol, to figure out why so many of these mattresses are slinging around the highway and killing people. We set up a little experiment with my producer, Lindsey, driving a car that has a mattress tied to the roof.

"Let me show you what people do," says Trooper Michael, pointing to a roll of twine.

"You take a mattress, you load it up on your SUV. The big box stores give out free twine for strapping it down. . . . It's not strong enough to hold a mattress on an SUV traveling at high speeds."

"But when the stores give this to you, you're thinking *it's from the store*. It must be safe," I say.

"Well, that's the misconception that people have."

So we tie up a mattress to the top of Lindsey's car. We do it the way most people do—a few simple knots, a few tugs, and it feels nice and tight. Then, on an abandoned runway at a regional airport, Lindsey gets behind the wheel. I follow her in Trooper Michael's car—he drives, thank God—to simulate what it would be like to follow her on a highway.

"Okay, here we go," Lindsey says. "I'm stepping on it."

Her car moves forward and we follow behind. The mattress flutters a bit in the wind.

Lindsey keeps her eye on the speedometer. "Twenty," she says.

At just *twenty* miles per hour, the mattress catches some wind and bends upward, shoving against the twine.

"Thirty, forty," she says.

The mattress is now flopping around like a flag in the wind. We're directly behind her in the chase car. I get nervous.

"Going forty-five . . . there it goes!" Lindsey says.

The mattress flips off her car. It rockets straight toward us, and the trooper deftly swerves out of the way, like a scene from a Jason Bourne film. If he had looked away for just two seconds? We could be dead.

Later, we salvage Lindsey's poor mattress, we lift it on top of her car again, and this time Trooper Michael shows us how to properly secure it.

"You should use ratchet straps," says the trooper, using them to cinch down the mattress. "Just like this one. For less than twenty bucks, you can pick this up at any big-box store." He takes a little hook, feeds it underneath the luggage rack, and then connects it to the strap. Then he's able to easily ratchet it so that it's cinched tight.

Again Lindsey drives off with the mattress. Twenty miles per hour, thirty, forty, fifty . . . seventy, no problem. The mattress doesn't budge.

"This will save lives," I say to the trooper, amazed at such a simple solution.

"Absolutely."

TWO KEY TAKEAWAYS: Don't use twine to tie a mattress to your car. It's cheap and it could snap and it could kill someone—not to mention you could lose your mattress (or bookcase).

If you're driving behind someone with a loosey-goosey mattress or cargo, stay well back, switch lanes, and then pass them. Once you're at a safe distance, call 911 and report the vehicle. (Don't worry, you're not being a nuisance or a tattletale—the troopers told us that they appreciate getting those calls, as it could ultimately save lives.)

How to Survive an Ice Skid

At times the road can seem like a video game, where you're dodging flying mattresses, other bad drivers, or a scary patch of ice. What should you do if you're caught in a skid?

I travel to Maryland to a specially designed ice-driving course, where Tom Pecoraro, a former cop and certified driving instructor, gives me the rules of the road.

With Pecoraro riding shotgun, I hop behind the wheel, speed up, and immediately hit a patch of ice and lose control.

"Whoa!" I yell out, panicking a bit, struggling to control the car. We spin around like a puck on an ice rink, just gliding across the road.

"So that was sixteen miles per hour."

"That's it?!"

Yep. At only sixteen miles per hour I lost control, as Pecoraro grimly reminds me, "and that's going to take you off the roadway or roll the car over or into another vehicle." And if I had been driving sixty miles per hour on a highway . . . well, "it's gonna be that many times worse."

Shaken, I hit the gas and again drive through the cold roads. Soon I hit more ice . . . and make a classic mistake. I jerk the wheel to the side and slam on the brakes.

"Two *worst* things you can do," says the former cop.

"What am I supposed to do?" I ask. That's not a rhetorical question. I have no idea.

"You're supposed to get off the brake," he explains. "Get off the accelerator, straighten the wheel, and then ride the skid out."

This goes against a driver's instinct, as it's human nature to pound the brakes when something goes wrong. But that could be deadly.

When you jam on the brakes and jerk the wheel, Pecoraro tells me, you're losing more control. And you need to have control during the skid.

THE TAKEAWAY: *Skid longer*, but be in control of it. Own the skid. This way you can steer away from things that are zooming toward you, and you'll regain control when you emerge from the skid. Is that terrifying? Yes. Is that potentially lifesaving? . . . another Yes.

3

WTF, I TRUSTED YOU!

WANT SOMETHING DONE RIGHT? *Do it yourself.* . . . . If only that worked in the real world. All of us need help. We get through life by trusting the experts—our doctors, our contractors, and the people who sell us things online. Society is built on this trust. But how reliable are these people? And what can we do to protect ourselves?

- Is Your Doctor Drunk?
- Movers Gone Wild
- The New Stranger Danger
- You Ruined My Prom
- Rossen vs. The Bank
- The Most Dangerous Eye Shadow Ever
- Can You Spare a Dollar to Help the Needy Children?
- I Can Read Your Fortune, Trust Me

Is Your Doctor Drunk?

Several years ago, Danielle and our kids were visiting my mother in Florida. I stayed back to work. (See, I'm dedicated.) Out of nowhere my mom fainted. Soon she got up and said she felt fine, but my wife was rattled by the fall.

"You need to go to the hospital," my wife urged her.

"No, I'm fine," my mom insisted.

I'm on the phone listening to what happened, screaming, *"Mom, go to the hospital!"* Eventually we convinced her to go to the ER for tests. They gave her a checkup and took scans and X-rays.

Before we knew it, a radiologist delivered surprising news. Pointing at the scan of Mom's lung, he says, "I don't know what caused you to faint, but this is something we need to biopsy." My mom could barely make it out. The scan showed a little white mark the size of her pinky fingernail. Needless to say, we all flipped out. And the results confirmed our worst fear.

Lung cancer. Even though she never smoked a day in her life.

But we "caught it early," the doctor explained, and it was only Stage 1, which meant that it hadn't spread and it could be safely removed.

Deep breath. So my mom went in for this "minor" surgery, which, we were told, was relatively routine. Then we received a phone call.

"I've got some bad news," said the doctor. *Oh God. What's he going to tell us?* My heart did a few flips. The doctor told us that, as a precaution, they tested her lymph node when doing the surgery. And they found a surprise. "It's Stage 3 lung cancer."

Stage 3. That can be a death sentence. It was the most devastating news I've ever heard. I dropped everything and hopped on a flight to be with my mom, and then hugged her, comforted her, and stayed with her.

Then we launched an intense search for the best doctor we could find. We researched and vetted and asked for recommendations. We were about to put my mom's life in the hands of a stranger, so I wanted to do my homework. We found a doctor we trusted, she got more tests, and then six months went by: It hadn't spread. Six months more went by: It *still* hadn't spread.

Every time she goes in for a checkup, we're white-knuckled and waiting for the report, and somehow, miraculously, *every time* it has come back with good news. As this book goes to press, my mom is still winning this battle with cancer.

This is all preamble to say that I have deeply personal reasons for trusting—and relying upon—our doctors and surgeons. We need them. We let doctors examine our brains, cut our bones with a knife, tell us what to eat and drink, and inspect every nook and cranny of our naked bodies. We trust them. We look up to them.

I personally vetted my mom's doctor. He's been amazing. Yet government data shows that at least 100,000 doctors and other health-care professionals working today—that's one in every ten— are abusing drugs or alcohol. Some of them have performed surgeries while stoned, and some are accused of crippling, paralyzing, and even killing their patients. Let me repeat that: *One in every ten doctors,* according to the government study, is abusing drugs and alcohol.

"There are doctors out there under the influence of prescription narcotics as we speak, putting patients at risk," says Dr. Stephen Loyd, a doctor from Tennessee. How does he know this? Because he was a stoned doctor. In a shockingly candid interview, he opened up and told me about his drug abuse.

"At my worst I was doing a hundred pills per day, Vicodin mainly," says Dr. Loyd.

"You were taking one hundred pills a day?"

"Yes."

"And you were seeing patients?"

"I was seeing patients."

How was this possible? How could this happen? I try to keep my composure, saying, "That's frightening."

"It's very frightening," he says, nodding. He explains that pills like Vicodin, which take the edge off an extraordinarily intense, stressful job, are, quite literally, right in front of doctors every day. They can just dip their hand in the cookie jar.

"I have access, and every friend I have is a doctor," says Loyd.

"They wrote you prescriptions?"

"Absolutely."

Part of me wonders, though, *Wouldn't I be able to tell if my doctor is high?* I've seen people on drugs—they're lost, scattered, unfocused. And doctors are usually sharp and incisive. I ask him about this; wouldn't I know if my doctor was high on pills?

"We'd like to think so," says Loyd, "but the truth of the matter is my patients didn't know I was using."

Dr. Loyd says that he has never been accused of harming a patient while under the influence, but other doctors have. Take the case of one doctor, a neurosurgeon, who once advertised himself in an infomercial as the best neurosurgeon in Dallas. He operated on a patient, Jeff Cheney, who, from the waist up, looks like a trim, healthy, fit, fortysomething.

Then I see him walk. Cheney walks with a broken limp, looking more like a brittle old man. When he climbs into the front seat of a car, he gingerly moves each leg, one at a time, using his hands and arms for assistance. Cheney didn't always walk like this. He went in for what the neurosurgeon called routine back surgery, and he came out partially paralyzed.

"You can barely walk?" I ask Cheney.

"Correct. And it's painful." Cheney speaks slowly, measuring his words, seemingly haunted by the experience. "It's my understanding that [the surgeon] was under the influence while performing surgeries."

"Cutting into people?"

"Yes, cutting into me."

I look at Cheney's legs again. They seem so out of sync with his healthy upper body. Cheney looks at me and says, "He turned me from a strong, healthy man into a crippled man."

Cheney is not the only one. A dozen other patients say that this same doctor botched their surgeries, too, turning some into paraplegics and quadriplegics, confining them to wheelchairs. According to lawsuits, two patients even *died* after their operations. In one recent deposition, one of the doctor's assistants testified that he often drank at work. One described a bottle of vodka under his desk. A friend described LSD and cocaine use.

And in the deposition, when the doctor was under oath, he kept repeating, "Take the Fifth."

Have you ever been under the influence of cocaine while you were taking care of a patient?

"I take the Fifth."

I request to interview him . . . denied. I visit his home in Dallas and knock on the door . . . no answer. Eventually I track him down on the phone, and he denies that he was drunk or stoned. He was never charged with any crime and the state medical board found no evidence he was on drugs or alcohol during surgeries, but his license was revoked because he violated the standard of care.

One doctor, however, is willing to open up and take responsibility: Doctor Loyd. He tells me he's been clean for more than a decade, and says that other physicians need to step up and follow his lead. As he speaks with me and reveals his Vicodin addiction to the world, and as he looks me in the eye, I realize that it's very rare, almost unprecedented, for us to sit across from someone who is so fully—and painfully—telling you the unfiltered truth. What he did was despicable. But now he's accepting it, owning it, and even sacrificing his reputation to help others learn the truth. In some ways I can't help but admire the guy. In fact, he's still practicing medicine.

I ask him point-blank: Don't you have a lot to lose by doing this interview?

He nods, acknowledging the risk. "If I've harmed a patient and the patient sees this interview and figures that I harmed them, then there is a price for me to pay for that."

"And you're willing to pay that price?"

"Of course," he says, nodding, dead sober. "Part of getting better with addictive disease is owning mistakes of the past."

That takes some guts. And it's another reminder that this guy, like all doctors, is a human being. We like to imagine that our doctors are demigods, or saints, or somehow floating above all the pesky matters of the flesh. Yet they have temptations and faults and weaknesses, just like the rest of us. We demand the impossible from them—fifteen hours straight doing heart surgery—unimaginable pressure and stress—then we want them to go home and be perfectly normal. Life doesn't always work like that.

SO HOW DO YOU CHECK UP ON YOUR DOCTOR?

1. Start at your state's medical board. Most have sites that let you search for your physician's license to confirm that they're in good standing, like fsmb.org. Some basic info is free, and for $9.95, on docinfo.org, you can look up additional background resources.

2. Check sites like healthgrades.com, lifescript.com, ratemds.com, and doctorscorecard.com that provide doctor reviews and links to state licensing boards.

3. A good old-fashioned Google search, which might turn up any lawsuits. (Or perhaps just the results of the doctor's seventh-grade soccer team.)

Theoretically, you could also run your own complete background check. If you're truly concerned, you can run a national criminal check to see if your doctor has convictions in other states. You could also check the National Sex Offender public website, and check both county and state criminal records.

And finally, if necessary, report your doctor. To file a complaint about your doctor, contact your state medical board.

Movers Gone Wild

Just how do we choose topics for Rossen Reports? Sometimes it's a story that's triggered by current events. Sometimes the idea comes to me in the shower. Sometimes the segments are requested by viewers, who e-mail us with tips. And of all the e-mails we get, this one is in the top three: Movers Gone Wild.

Maybe this shouldn't be so surprising. Think about it. When you hire a moving company, you give them literally every possession you own, and then they can take it away and hold it hostage. Thirty-five million Americans move every year, and authorities say that complaints against movers are on the rise.

Exhibit A: Ashley Kenner and Mike Gorokhovsky, who hired a moving company to truck their stuff from Florida to Colorado. They contacted our office to say that their stuff was being held hostage, and asked if we could help.

We said yes. Feeling a bit like a private eye, I fly to their home in Colorado and they welcome me inside. The three-bedroom house has beautiful new hardwood floors, good lighting, high ceilings, and . . . nothing else. I look around the barren living room. No furniture. Nothing.

We awkwardly make introductions. "We normally do interviews sitting on chairs," I say, sitting cross-legged on the floor. "This is a new one."

"Yeah," says Ashley. "We don't have chairs."

I take a little tour and find just one lonely piece of furniture, their air mattress. Damn. I'd seen better-furnished dorm rooms. They then show me their moving contract—it clearly stated that for $1,773 their stuff would be moved from Florida to Colorado within fourteen to twenty-one business days. But that was *two months* ago.

Ashley says that she called the company every day. They never responded. So it's no surprise that the company was under investigation by the federal government. They had *dozens* of complaints for pickup and delivery problems, overcharging, and holding people's stuff hostage.

My team tracks down the company at a nondescript office park in Fort Lauderdale. We called and asked them for an interview; they declined. (I get a lot of that.) But I show up in person anyway for a friendly little chat.

"You're not allowed in here," one of the employees tells me.

"Do the names Mike Gorokhovsky and Ashley Kenner ring a bell?" I ask.

"No."

"Customers who say—"

"Can you step outside?" they ask.

"You've been holding their stuff hostage for more than two months."

"Can you step outside?" (I get a lot of that, too.)

Then they slam the door in my face. (Yep, I definitely get a lot of that.)

The company later sent us an e-mail saying there had been "no runaround" with the couple, and that for two months they didn't know where to deliver their belongings, because on the initial estimate it was listed as going into storage in Colorado. (The couple denies this.)

"Just to be clear, do you want your stuff in storage?" I ask Ashley.

"We never wanted our stuff in storage."

"You told them multiple times where you live and where to bring it?"

"Yes."

And then, voilà, a day later, in another whopper of a coincidence, the moving company finally delivers their stuff. (And perhaps shamed by the TV pressure, they even give the couple a full refund.)

In her kitchen, Ashley happily unpacks her boxes of dishes, no longer stuck using paper plates. "We can have some champagne now!"

"Drink up," I tell her.

I love a happy ending as much as the next guy. Of course, not every exploited customer will have a TV crew to lobby their case. But there are a few things that everyone can do to avoid getting hoodwinked. Most important, always get an estimate *in person*, at your home, where they can see your stuff and the scope of the job. If you get the estimate over the phone, they can later jack up the price and say something like, "Oh, well, the job was much bigger than you described." Make them see it in person before they give you a quote.

And when you think about it, even the word "estimate" is a bit tricky. You think of it as the actual price, but they think of it as a ballpark guess that might change . . . and funny how it always changes higher. That's why whenever I negotiate a move, I always have them add the words "not to exceed." This locks in the price. I'm even willing to pay a bit *more* in the contract to lock in the estimate; in other words, I'd rather have a contract that says "not to exceed $2,100" than an "estimate of $2,000." And finally, before you hire anyone, look up their history online.

The New Stranger Danger

"Never talk to strangers." We've been told that since we were babies. It's a cliché: *Stranger Danger*. I'm almost embarrassed to give my own kids that advice, as it feels a little corny, and it's the oldest parenting advice on the planet. It seems so obvious.

The truth is that most parents *do* give their little kids an effective Stranger Danger talk. And the kids even listen.

But then something funny happens.

The kids grow up. The kids turn into teenagers. And the teenagers think that they're smart, savvy, and untouchable. This is why, paradoxically, *teenagers* are more at risk of being kidnapped than toddlers. In 2013, for example, seventy-two young adults ages eighteen to twenty-five were reported abducted by strangers. It's chilling. Even more surprising? It's easy for predators to lure these teenagers into a van.

To find out, I posed as a "stranger" to see if college students could be lured into a van. I didn't think it would work. *Teenagers aren't that dumb,* I thought. We almost nixed the experiment, as I was sure that no one would bite.

"It's not gonna work," I say to Josh, my longtime and trusty producer.

"You'd be surprised."

"No one's gonna do it!"

Yet Josh convinces me to pose as "Rob Reynolds," a reality-TV show producer. You haven't heard of Rob Reynolds? He's the head of RR Productions, and he's looking to cast some college kids in his show. (I made up this sleazeball—but the kids didn't know that.) He drives a dark van. He wears a black jacket and a black baseball cap.

On a gray winter morning, I drive Rob's creepy van to a nearby university, parking it in the middle of campus. The whole thing feels icky, but hey, it's the only way we could find out what the college kids would actually do. Make no mistake, "going undercover" feels weird. It makes me nervous when I pretend to be someone else. Yet it's for the greater good, and sometimes, as a journalist, I have to do it to expose a larger truth.

Feeling uncomfortable and sketchy, I pose as Rob Reynolds and watch the teenagers stroll around campus with their books, backpacks, and mugs of coffee.

My team whipped up some fake business cards for the flashy sounding "RR Productions," complete with a snazzy logo. (RR, naturally, also stands for Rossen Reports.) I lug around a home video camera that looks like it is straight from the nineties, the kind of bulky gear you could fit a VHS tape into.

"Hi, we're casting a reality show about college students. Are you interested?" I call out to various students, feeling like a creep.

One student, maybe nineteen years old, walks by in a gray hoodie. He tells me his name is Anthony. I ask him to get in the van to look over the reality-show paperwork.

"I'm not getting in a car, man," Anthony says.

"You don't want to get in the car?"

"No."

"Are you sure? It'll just take two minutes."

"Yeah, I'm fine, man."

Anthony walks off. I shoot a look at Josh, who's hiding in a nearby car, watching everything. *See? No one's biting.*

We try again with another college student, this time a young woman.

"I don't feel comfortable getting in a car," she says. "My mother taught me well."

Zero for two.

Then we meet Nicole, a young student.

"Hey Nicole . . . can you just fill out this form?" I point inside the van. "It's warm in there. Have a seat."

"Okay," Nicole says, smiling, clearly wanting to impress this reality-show producer. My heart sinks a little. It was so easy. Too easy. I try not to think of my own young children. Would they, too, want to impress Rob Reynolds?

Nicole scoots to the backseat of the van, filling out a form on the clipboard. The fake form is designed to capture their personal information—name, address, even Social Security number.

"Why would you want to be on a reality show?" I ask, filming her with my camera.

"I think it's really cool!" Nicole says. "I see, like, stars like Kim Kardashian, and people like that, that just kind of have fun."

As Nicole jots down her info, I say one more thing, almost as an afterthought.

"By the way, can I grab your phone real quick?" I ask casually.

"Yeah," Nicole says, handing it to me.

Once again, the parent inside me cries out in pain. *Nicole.* I realize that for these college students, casting a reality show is like candy. Toddlers can be lured by candy made of sugar, and teens can be lured by candy made of fame. And these are college kids. Smart kids.

We do the same routine with another kid—he, too, hands over his phone, blinded by the chance of becoming famous. And then two teenage girls enter the van, roommates, and they giggle and laugh and even joke about the risk of getting kidnapped.

"If you . . . drive off, I'll be very upset!" says one of the girls, laughing.

"I would *cut you* if you drove off, no offense," says the other with a smile.

With each college student, afterward, we told them who we really were. They were shaken. They couldn't believe that they had been duped so easily.

"I was able to get you into that van," I tell Nicole. "You didn't ask for my ID. You even handed your cell phone over to me, no questions asked."

"I know, crazy," she says, a little shell-shocked, her reality-show dream dying, replaced instead by a very different sense of reality. "This will teach me a lot about . . . being more aware."

I nod, and she walks off. I take off my Rob Reynolds creep hat. The episode haunts me. Later, to help make sense of this, I speak with the one man who truly knows this world: John Walsh, the creator and host of *America's Most Wanted*, and the nation's foremost expert on child abduction, after his son was abducted and killed by a stranger.

"I think every college kid thinks they're bulletproof and immortal," John Walsh tells me.

"And that's something a kidnapper can use?"

"Absolutely."

And these kids actually *got in the van*. I hesitate to ask . . . but what could happen then?

"Now he can rape you, beat you, kill you, drop your body off, do whatever he wants," says Walsh. "You're on his turf. You're in his lair."

It's chilling. But it taught me that Stranger Danger is more than a cliché, and it needs to be told to kids when they're two years old, three years old, fourteen, nineteen, and every damn year until they retire. Because Rob Reynolds was make-believe. Others like him are real. And they're out there.

You Ruined My Prom

My young daughters Skyler and Sloane are already dreaming of their wedding day. Many little girls do. And when these young women get to high school, many view prom as a "mini–wedding day," their first real experience with a fancy event. Often they save up their money, work extra hours at a job, or beg their parents for a loan— all for a prom dress.

To a group of despicable scammers, these young women are something else entirely: targets. "Prom is the Oscars to a high school kid," says Kimberly Gambale, owner of Diane & Company, a boutique that sells prom gowns. Kimberly has seen more and more young women get duped into buying fake dresses online. "At least three to four times a week we're faced with girls who have been scammed by online websites."

In a bit of irony, the fake websites are very, very good. The text on the fake sites reads just like the text on the actual designer sites, the images look identical, the logos look identical.

"I was working for months to save up the money," says Alexandra, a high school student. She found a gorgeous dress that normally costs $400. One website—which looked reputable— sold it for 25 percent off. *Done and done.* She pulled the trigger and was ecstatic. "My immediate reaction was, oh my gosh, this is awesome," Alexandra tells me. "The dress that I love, it's beautiful, and it's at a great price, so it's going to make Mom happy, too."

It came in the mail and she freaked out. That's when I came by and she showed me the dress. I would have burst out laughing if this wasn't a real hardship—with real financial and emotional consequences. The dress is a cheap knockoff. Look, I'm no expert on gowns, so when I say "cheap knockoff," I don't mean that the stitching is a little bit frayed, or that the emeralds have just a touch less sheen. I mean this: It looked like crap. Even to my naïve eyes. It was the wrong color, the wrong size, and it looked like something that my daughter Sloane would have made for her school art project . . . if she were blindfolded.

Alexandra leaves the room to try it on, returns, and then, her face in pain, seems on the verge of tears. "The lining is so itchy," she says. "The dress feels cheap and I feel like I look cheap in it." Alexandra shows me the website where she bought the dress, and in the photo, it has a lovely arrangement of beads. Her actual dress? The good news is that it came with beads. The bad news is that the beads were not even attached to the dress, but came in a separate plastic bag, and they also gave her a *sewing kit*. Yep, that's right, they treated her dress like IKEA furniture. "Do they expect me to sew this on?" asks Alexandra.

To some people this is all a joke, but it's also a crime, and the stakes are real. "It's a huge problem," says Dusty Hill, the president of Sherri Hill (a top gown designer), a company that takes the problem so seriously, in fact, that it hired two full-time investigators to hunt down the counterfeit sites. He knows it's not an easy problem to fix, as counterfeit sites are like that arcade game Whac-A-Mole, where you knock one down, and then another one pops up. "It's going to be an ongoing fight," Hill admits.

So how do you protect yourself, or your daughters, against this kind of hustling?

TWO KEY WORDS: *authorized dealer.*

Experts say that if you find a good deal online, then call the actual company that makes the dress and ask, "I'm on this website right now, is it an authorized dealer?" Many are, and if the site is legit, the company should be able to tell you. Many top prom dress designers also have a list of authorized retailers right on their websites. (Also? That's a good tip for buying anything pricey online that might be fake, from jewelry to designer watches.) It doesn't hurt to double-check.

"I didn't feel beautiful," Alexandra tells me, holding up the cheap frayed fabric. "And you're supposed to feel beautiful at prom."

Rossen vs. The Bank

I'll come right out and say it: I'm too lazy to count all of my loose change. It's a hassle, right? My family keeps our change in a plastic jar that's larger than a gallon of milk, and whenever it fills up, we take it to one of those automatic coin-counting machines. I've always taken it on blind faith that these machines accurately tabulate the nickels and dimes.

But am I really the one getting nickeled and dimed?

I enlist the help of my dogged producers, Josh and Jovanna, to take it old-school and meticulously count a small fortune's worth of pennies, nickels, dimes, and quarters. It's thankless work. For hours Josh has the mind-numbing task of sticking pennies into the little sleeves, and he takes it like a champ.

Many (many) hours later, we now have sacks of coins that each total $300.00. We counted them to the penny. Then we lug these bags—they're heavier than you would think!—to a bunch of different coin machines to test their accuracy.

First stop: those popular Coinstar machines that you see at the grocery store. Jovanna pours the coins into the bucket and it counts . . . and counts . . . and counts . . . and then the sensor flashes a score, almost like it does on *The Price Is Right*: $300.00. Nailed it! Coinstar is accurate to the penny. We then test another Coinstar: $300.00.

So far, so good. Next up is one of the nation's largest banks, TD Bank, where we tested their machines at several different branches.

I pour the coins into the first TD Bank machine and it chugs and chugs and counts and counts and finally it spits out the value . . . $299.95. Huh. I suppose that losing a nickel isn't going to kill me, but still, shouldn't it be exactly accurate?

Then we head to the second TD Bank machine . . . $299.47. Again, a difference of 53 cents is not going to make or break anyone's mortgage payment, but still . . .

The next one is off by even more: $296.27. Okay. Now we're talking about a real difference. Also, is it a coincidence that in every single case, the value the machine calculates is *lower* than $300, never higher?

We head to the final TD Bank machine. Jovanna, grateful to finally be done with these coins, pours the sack into the machine and watches it count and count and count . . . and it spits out a value of $256.90. *Are you kidding me?* It's off by more than $43. That's a lot of money. In New York that's enough money to buy almost three beers.

So I speak to the manager at TD Bank and explain the problem.

"Okay," says the bank manager, a thirtysomething guy wearing a gray suit.

"The machine gave us an inaccurate count. In fact, the machine gave us more than $43 less than what we brought in," I say, and I feel a little bad for the manager, because clearly it wasn't *his* fault.

"I'll look into your concern, absolutely," he says.

Soon we hear from TD Bank headquarters, who says that they were disappointed with our experience, that they place a premium on their integrity, and that they "clean and test [the machines] twice daily."

"I'm shocked," says Edgar Dworsky, founder of *Consumer World*. "You think of a bank being a hundred percent accurate. If you're a penny off paying your mortgage, they're going to slap you with a late fine. And here they are, giving you less for your money? Not right."

As a result of our investigation, TD Bank pulled the machines out of circulation . . . permanently. Then something even more surprising happened: People were *pissed*. At *me*. One guy approached me on the street and said, "Thanks to you, now I have to roll all my own coins. Get a life, assh$&#!"

Another angry viewer: "Now what should I do with my loose change?!"

I was a little baffled. "But they were taking your money! Don't you want your money?!"

"I can't spend the loose change," the guy said.

I realized that sometimes people are willing to take a financial hit—even if they're being cheated—for the sake of convenience. As a local cable anchor said on-air after the machines were pulled, "Thanks for *nothing*, Jeff Rossen."

Um . . . you're welcome, America?

The Most Dangerous
Eye Shadow Ever

Remember how they found mold in my own kitchen, my own bathroom, my own washing machine? The findings haunted me. For starters, this is one of the ugliest words in the English language: *mold*. Just that one itty-bitty syllable feels gross, rotten, and makes you want to wash your hands. *Mold.* And when you discover that you have mold in your house, you're worried that it will ooze and spread and that the walls will crumble, the foundation will buckle, and that you (and maybe your kids) will somehow get sick.

So if you see a dark spot that might be mold, it's only natural to call a mold inspector. But are these guys legit? Will they try to rip you off? "I think it's happening a lot more than people think," says Howard White, a mold remediation supervisor with Maxons Restorations. "Typically, they're preying on people's fears, and people just want to know that their homes are clean and safe."

It's time for another contractor experiment.

We rent a house in suburban New Jersey, and first we hire two reputable environmental testing companies to inspect the house from top to bottom, testing for mold and moisture. The house passes with flying colors—it's clean.

Then we get a little sneaky. Our expert dabs black eye shadow in three spots around the house—a little black scuff that might scare the average homeowner, but would obviously *not be mold* to any legit inspector.

My producer, Kelly, poses as a concerned homeowner. She calls a parade of mold inspectors to examine these mysterious dark spots and, as always, we use hidden cameras to keep tabs on the operation.

Kelly shows the first inspector the dark marks in the basement, playing the part of an anxious mom.

"My son's down here all the time," says Kelly. "I see spots like this and I just wanted to get them checked out."

The inspector looks at the eye shadow. Examines it closely. "I'm in the job to sell basement waterproofing and mold remediation," he says, "I don't think you need us."

He adds that if the spots *are* mold, they're so minor that Kelly can clean them herself.

Another contractor confirms: "It's not mold." So does a third.

The first three inspectors are on the up-and-up. You have nothing to worry about. The end.

Kidding. By now you know better—our results were about to take a darker turn. The next inspector, who looks a bit like Turtle from *Entourage*, gives us the verdict just two minutes after stepping inside the basement.

"Definitely mold," says Turtle. "There's no question about it."

He tells our concerned mom that not only does she have mold, but also water damage, and that to fix the problem, he'll need to *cut out Sheetrock and spray with chemicals.*

But it gets even better! Turtle says that, typically, he's not supposed to give a verdict until he officially performs a test, but as a courtesy to the mom—and because he's such a great guy—he'll skip the formalities. "You don't need to pay for a test because it's definitely, I mean, this is definitely mold."

It's worth remembering the obvious: The entire *purpose* of a "test" is to, well, test to determine whether the black mark is actually mold or whether it's something like, say, black eye shadow. If a contractor ever helpfully offers to let you "skip" a test on a harmless-looking mark, that could be a scam tactic.

Turtle's price: $1,050.

"Hi, Jeff Rossen from NBC News," I say, coming out of hiding.

"How you doing?" he asks, sensing that he's now in a world of hurt.

"Are you a trained and certified mold technician?"

"Yes."

"So you're telling me that you thought that was mold?" I ask.

A slight pause. Turtle switches tactics, asking me, "Do you feel good about yourself?"

"No, not at all," I say, amazed at the dude's nerve. "I hate that you were trying to charge her $1,000 for a problem that doesn't exist."

"It's funny," he says, "because there's a lot of companies out there who are very dishonest." He shakes his head like he's the victim, and before he leaves he says once again to me, "You should feel good about yourself."

Turtle, alas, is not the only unscrupulous mold contractor. Kelly calls more inspectors and we get more of the same.

"Yes, that's definitely black mold," says the next inspector. "I don't think you need to test. It's a waste of money."

He wants to charge $1,200.

And the charade continues. The next contractor doesn't waste any time, clearly spotting a fat payday. "That's black mold," he says with a crisp note of authority.

"That's black mold?" asks Kelly.

"Absolutely. Absolutely. You've got water in here. I can still smell the dampness from it. You know something, it's not healthy. It's not healthy."

This guy says we have serious water leaks causing the mold. (Remember, two reputable companies checked this house for mold and moisture and gave it a clean bill of health.)

"I'm going to break out the floor," the inspector says, radiating confidence and expertise. "I'm going to take a saw. I'm going to pull all this molding off."

"How big of a problem do you think I have here?" asks Kelly, still playing the part of the chump.

"Well, I think you have a $10,000 problem."

Specifically, the expert crunches the numbers and rings up a problem of exactly $10,871 to install a new drain system. Suddenly I'm starting to miss ol' Turtle.

Now it's time to end this farce.

"Hi, I'm Jeff Rossen with NBC News."

"Hi, Jeff Rossen with NBC News," the guy says with surprising cheerfulness. "I've seen you on television. Wow, this is really interesting. I thought you were on television."

"We're on TV right now."

Surprise! In the end, five out of eight mold contractors, more than half, wanted to charge Kelly for work that experts said she did not need. "It questions the integrity of my entire industry when

I see people like this," says Howard White, the mold remediation supervisor. He looks glum and I can't blame him.

A takeaway:

\\\\|///,

Experts say mold contractors should always do a complete visual inspection.

///|\\\\

If your home has clear visible mold that is growing in size, or a serious water problem, or if your family is getting sick, those are legit warning signs that you may have mold, and in that extreme case, a contractor might not need to do any testing. Either way, no matter what, it doesn't hurt to get a second opinion when somebody comes in and says, "Give me money." Because life is hard enough without these rip-offs.

Can You Spare a Dollar to Help the Needy Children?

I want to tell you about a charity called *Raise the Kids Alliance*. They do good work. The folks at *Raise the Kids* give money to children with medical problems, helping those in need. Their work is important. For less than the price of one cup of coffee, you could help a child with a serious medical disease.

Yet there's only one tiny problem with *Raise the Kids Alliance*: I made it up. Criminals can do the same thing. I've exposed a lot of bad guys over the years—people like crooked contractors, dirty salesmen, and shady online retailers. But this is the lowest of the low: people who set up fake charities.

They prey on your generosity. They pounce on your guilt. They tug on your heartstrings . . . and then they pocket your cash. You might ask, okay, but does this *really* happen? Isn't it easy to spot the fake ones?

I wanted to find out. So, as an experiment, I print up some fake brochures for *Raise the Kids Alliance*, along with some fake signs, and even some sad, heartbreaking photos of young children who clearly need your help. The kids aren't fake: They're photos of my kids (Blake and Sloane) refusing to smile. To make them look extra glum, I asked them to think about doing their homework.

I lug all this fake charity paraphernalia to Hoboken, New Jersey, and set up a table on a busy sidewalk. I begin approaching strangers in the most gentle, nonthreatening voice I can, saying things like, "Would you like to help the children?"

Immediately I feel like a fraud. *No one's gonna fall for this.* I have no clue what *Raise the Kids Alliance* actually does. If someone were to press me, I would be unable to back up my flimsy lie.

"Excuse me, ma'am, hi, are you interested in helping children in need?" I ask one lady.

"Sure," she says, and pulls out her wallet without a second thought. *Wow. That was easy.*

"Would you like to help the children?" I ask someone else. "Even just a dollar or two helps."

The woman pulls out her wallet. "We have to help children, right?"

I brought a large fishbowl to collect the donations, and soon it begins to fill with crumpled dollars. I can't believe it. This is insanely easy. People start giving. And giving. And giving. One guy cracks open his wallet and pulls out a *twenty*.

"You're doing something *nice!*" one woman tells me.

One young woman approaches the table, holding a cup of healthy (and expensive) green juice. She, too, soon plunks some cash into the bowl, laughs, and says, "Why not? I'm walking around with a six-dollar juice."

Almost *everyone* seems to give—men, women, old, young. People of all ethnicities and backgrounds. I've finally found something that truly unites America: fake charities. Almost no one asks any questions.

"What organization is it?" one guy asks.

"Raise the Kids Alliance," I say. "We help children with medical problems."

"Is it any specific problem?" he asks.

Uh-oh . . . "Um . . . many problems, many diseases, many issues," I say, my fraud basically exposed.

But this *still* doesn't deter the guy! "You gotta do it for the kids," he says, and then donates. One man approaches, sees the sign and the sad photos of the young children in need (Blake and Sloane) and then he pulls out his wallet and donates.

"Thank you so much, sir," I say to him, but then I add, "There is one other thing I want to tell you." I let him in on the secret, explaining that this is a stunt, and that this is not a real charity.

The guy shakes his head, baffled, and can't believe he has just been played. "I am in the military as well, too," he says.

"Thank you for your service," I say, shaking his hand. He then thanks me for playing him.

Even a man trained by the military was fooled. (Incidentally, I told everyone the truth. Once they donated, I gave each person the option of getting their money back, or letting me donate the cash to a real, honest-to-God children's charity. Everyone insisted that we donate the cash to a good cause.)

But maybe I could up the ante?

Now I try another tactic of frauds and hucksters: *the upsell.* I had also brought a few adorable teddy bears and displayed them on the table.

After one guy drops some money into the jar I tell him, "For an additional five dollars, we will buy a teddy bear for a child, and deliver it right to them." He takes the bait and kicks in five bucks more.

When another generous person strolls by, after she gives a few bucks, I peer into her wallet and see she has more to spare. "I saw you have a five in there . . ." I say, really pressing my luck.

"Yeah."

I tell her that for just five dollars, we are going to buy a teddy bear and deliver it to a child.

"All right."

Yet not everyone was so trusting. One middle-aged guy, tall, wearing a black T-shirt and pushing a baby stroller, gives me a hard, penetrating stare. "What's your website?" he asks.

"We're Raise the Kids Alliance," I say, with a little less confidence in my voice.

He pulls out his smartphone and begins to google my nonexistent charity.

"Dot something?" he asks.

"Dot com," I say, feeling like George Costanza caught in a lie.

"*Com?* Wow, that's interesting. Are you a nonprofit or . . . ?"

"We're a charity that helps children," I say, flailing.

"You're not answering my question." He walks off, disgusted, and he *should* be disgusted. (This guy did it right!)

Soon I get another hardball question from another skeptical passerby. She looks at me, looks at our booth, googles me, and asks, "Are you also known as the Alliance for Children's Rights?"

"We are Raise the Kids Alliance," I say, repeating just about the only line I know.

"Do you have your 501(c)(3)?" she asks.

Whoa! She just brought out the big guns! "No, we do not," I say, wishing I could slap her a high five. Yet I stay in character and say, "We are trying to get it."

"You're *trying* to get it?"

"A lot of bureaucracy . . ."

She (wisely) refuses to donate. She did everything right: asked about the 501(c)(3), asked about a website, and checked on her smartphone to ensure we're legit.

THAT'S THE TAKEAWAY HERE: Of course we want to give to charity, and of course we *should* help worthy causes, but it's smart to do a quick background check. It only takes a few seconds.

Yet we had one final task in our little experiment. Remember that fishbowl, the one that filled with cash? In less than three hours, amazingly, that bowl collected $667 from people on the street. We took this money to a real charity, called the Cure 4 The Kids Foundation, which is a real organization with a real 501(c)(3). They help kids with diseases, including pediatric cancer.

Walking inside this clinic, I head to a classroom full of smiling, eager, and innocent children. I'm carrying a giant cardboard poster under my arm.

"You're probably wondering," I say to the kids, "What's a grown man doing with a big piece of cardboard?"

"Yeah!" the kids say in unison.

Then I reveal what I'm holding—one of those giant oversized checks, the kind that radiates hope and promise. The check is written for $1,334 . . . the original $667 we raised in the fishbowl, matched dollar for dollar because, well, why not?

The kids cheer. And remember those teddy bears we said we would give to the children? Not a lie. I unveil a cart behind me that's filled with teddy bears—one for every child, exactly as promised. I toss teddy bear after teddy bear into the class, soaking up their laughter and joy. It feels good to give, and it feels even better when you *know* it's going to the right place. Three sites I recommend: foundationcenter.org, give.org, and charitywatch.org.

I Can Read Your Fortune, Trust Me

I am going to show you a trick. Thanks to my clairvoyant powers, I can see your eyeballs reading this very book, and I can peer into the depths of your soul.

You have an aura that tells me that you . . . woke up today, yes? I thought so. You like to eat breakfast in the morning? Yes, yes, I suspected as much. I sense that you have a job, yet your boss, at times, can be annoying, and you hunger for a promotion. I also feel a tinge of *sadness* coming from you, and I sense that you once experienced a painful loss? It still gnaws at you, sometimes beneath the surface.

Sigh.

As you can probably guess by now, I'm a bit of a skeptic when it comes to psychics and fortune-tellers. You know the ones I'm talking about, right? (My crystal ball tells me you do.) They advertise palm readings for ten dollars, or they'll divine your future from a deck of tarot cards, or maybe they'll ask you to clutch some rare crystals. So just how accurate are they?

Since they have their own secrets and tricks, I decide to use a few tricks of my own. I visit several of these shops, but I come armed with hidden cameras. I'm wearing one in the button of my shirt. Posing as a regular guy who's curious about his future—in fairness, that's *not* an act—I enter the small room of a tarot-card reader, then sit down at a table. A flickering candle illuminates the psychic's face.

"Shuffle the cards," she instructs me.

So I do. She considers me, thinks about my aura, and then says, "You have a positive energy, but there's a lot of negative people around your work, and also people you socialize with."

Take that, coworkers! (Also: Is there anyone on the planet who would *not* identify with that analysis? We all like to think of ourselves as the "positive source of energy," the hero.)

Then she drops a bombshell.

"In January, a new career," she says.

"A new career for me in January?"

"Yes."

(Let's hope NBC never sees this.)

We head to the second psychic, and now I'm curious about my

love life. As she flips the tarot cards I ask her, "What is it saying about my relationships?"

"Hmmmm," she says, mulling over the cards.

"Marriage? Kids?"

"No, not marriage right now. But it does show a relationship for you happening next year."

"A relationship next year, but no marriage?" I ask her, just to make sure I heard her correctly.

"No marriage, not for right now."

Yet there's just one person who might disagree with this prediction: my lovely wife, Danielle. Ninety-nine times out of a hundred, the psychic's line would work like a charm. Ninety-nine times out of a hundred, people would listen to her soothing prediction—a relationship next year, but not marriage—and feel a renewed sense of hope. They would feel more confident. It just so happens, though, that in this one case out of a hundred, I had removed my wedding ring and stuffed it in my pocket.

I politely thank her—trying not to crack up laughing—leave her shop, and then return to properly introduce myself.

"Hi, again," I say, now in my news-anchor voice. "I'm actually from NBC News and we're doing a story about psychic readings."

"Oh my God."

"Are these readings not accurate?"

"No, they are," she says.

"But I'm married."

"I understand that," she says, without missing a beat. "And sometimes within a reading, it'll pick up a *past* life."

"That's not what you told me, though," I say, weirdly happy that I found a cool wife in a previous life, too.

"Listen, if you want your money back I will give it back to you," she says, shielding her face from the camera. "If you don't, then you need to get out of my store."

Fair enough. We head for a third psychic, and this time she asks me to hold some crystals in my hand. The other psychics had relied upon tarot cards, but crystals, clearly, are the key to unlocking the secrets of my soul.

Again my love life comes up.

"What I do see is that you haven't met your soul mate yet, but you will," she says.

Ouch! Sorry, Danielle, I know we've been happily married for eight years, but these crystals say I should look around.

"When do you think I'll meet her?" I ask.

"Somewhere between [now and] March is coming in as the most positive time for you to actually meet this person."

"Will I get married next year?"

"Well, she's not going to be ready to be married in the same year, but I do see that the following year, yes."

She's really given this scenario a lot of thought. I try to clarify: "So I'll be ready to get married to her next year, but she's going to want to wait . . . to marry me?"

"Exactly . . . And it also shows me she has an accent. She's not American."

"My soul mate has an accent, you're feeling? She's not American?"

"No."

(Danielle, I *promise* that I do not spend every March looking for exotic women with accents who don't want to get married until the following year.)

The fortune-teller then looks at my hand. I'm still holding the crystals. "If you make a fist," she says, "I'll tell you how many kids you're going to have."

I make a fist, clutching the cold stones.

"Two," she says.

"I'm going to have two kids?"

"Yeah."

"What are the sexes?"

"Well, it seems like you're having boys."

"All boys?"

"That's it."

So close! Except that my two daughters might disagree.

Now here's the truly strange thing . . . there's something that I actually *am* nervous about, and that's being told that I will die young. I can't explain it. I've always feared that I will die young. There's nothing logical or rational about this anxiety. When we approach one of the tarot-card readers, even though I suspect the whole operation is rigged, and even though part of me wants to snicker, I actually feel a pinprick of fear when she flips the cards.

"How long do you think I'm going to live?" I ask.

She looks at me. She looks at the cards. And all of the hidden cameras and the jokes are far from my mind. *How long am I going to live? Tell me. Tell me.*

"I can see that your lifeline is very strong," she says.

Phew.

But maybe that's a fluke? I ask the same question of another fortune-teller. "How long am I going to live?"

She, too, looks at the cards and looks deep into my eyes. "The cards indicate to me that you're going to live a long life."

I'm embarrassed at how happy this makes me. Maybe they're a

sham, and maybe the whole thing is a gimmick, but there *is* something thrilling about hearing the news that you desperately wanted to hear. I ask the same question to a *third* fortune-teller. How long will I live?

"You have a healthy life ahead of you," she says, smiling.

"Long?"

"Very long."

Thank God. My new soul mate will be pleased.

4

IT'S ALL FUN AND
GAMES . . . UNTIL . . .

MAYBE YOU'RE SKIING OR SNOWSHOEING, and suddenly you fall through thin ice. Or maybe your parasail snaps. Or your ticket to a music concert is fake. These are all wildly different moments in life, but they have one thing in common: They *start* with something innocent and even fun, and then, without warning, it takes a darker turn. . . .

- ◎   . . . You Fall Through Thin Ice
- ◎   . . . Your Parasail Snaps
- ◎   . . . Your Concert Tickets Are Fake
- ◎   . . . You Realize: "I'm Drunk"
- ◎   . . . You're Buried Alive
- ◎   . . . Your Carnival Game Is Rigged

. . . You Fall Through Thin Ice

Here's the problem with thin ice: It looks exactly like solid ice. This is why every winter, across America, skiers and kids and dog walkers and sledders—most of them laughing, goofing around, having a jolly time—suddenly plunge through the ice, sink into the cold waters, and many freeze to death or drown.

These people aren't stupid. It's not like they said, "Hey, I'm going to tempt fate and tiptoe across this frozen pond!" Ice can look *just like solid ground.* Snow-covered ice looks the same as snow-covered dirt. White is white. In the era of smartphone videos, we've seen horrifying footage of normal people going about their wintry business, maybe dreaming about hot cocoa, and then, *CRACK*, their life is in jeopardy. Sometimes rescuers can yank them to safety. Sometimes they slip and fall. And sometimes their *friends* try to save them, but then the friends, too, fall through the ice.

So how do you survive this? Steeling myself for another freezing experiment, I travel to Maine to consult with certified rescuers, who will teach me how to stay alive when falling through thin ice.

The first thing they do is strap me in a thick, yellow wet suit that goes from my neck to my toes. It looks like a yellow hazmat suit, those things scientists wear when working with plutonium. (*What have you gotten yourself into, Rossen?*) An ambulance is on standby, just thirty feet away. (*Why do so many of my work days involve ambulances?*) Rescue trainer Gerry Dworkin, clad head-to-foot in his own yellow wet suit, guides me toward a frozen pond.

Did I mention it's cold outside? Freezing. And this is *aboveground.* Dworkin, perhaps questioning my sanity, directs me to a section of the ice. I hesitate. Is this really a good idea?

Think about the last time you climbed up a really high diving board. Remember that moment of fear as you climbed up the ladder? And then, as you stood at the edge of the diving board, a knot formed in your stomach and you thought about climbing back down. Now multiply that fear by a thousand.

Screw it. I keep walking.

Crack. Crack. Uh-oh. Crack. I fall in. Instantly I'm freezing cold—even in my yellow hazmat suit—and I have only a split-second to execute:

\\\ | / / /

SURVIVAL TIP 1: Put your hand over your mouth and nose the moment you hit the water. This is critical. This is life and death.

/ / / | \ \ \

"If you take a breath of cold water, it's going to shut down your airway and you're going to stop breathing," Dworkin explains. That sounds bad. "Cardiac arrest will follow shortly after that."

Thank God I remembered to cover my face, and when my head bobs to the surface, the cold wind licking my cheeks, I grab hold of the edge of the ice.

"If I wasn't wearing this suit right now, what would be happening?" I ask Dworkin, who stands a few feet away.

The water is dark and deadly. "If you just had regular clothing, they would become very heavy, very quickly, and it's going to suck you right under the ice."

And oh, by the way, once you're trapped under the ice, your chance of survival plummets. So don't do that.

With my body still submerged in the freezing water, I hold on to the edge of the ice, literally grasping for dear life. It's tough to get a grip.

"I'm a good swimmer, and this is harder than I thought," I somehow say as I'm flailing.

That brings us to:

SURVIVAL TIP 2: Carry ice picks.

I know it's not realistic for you to bring these with you wherever you go, but if you're headed outdoors near a frozen lake or pond, take the ice picks with you. The metal spikes dig in so you can pull yourself out. They only cost a few dollars at outdoor stores, and fit in your pocket. No bigger than a pen.

I stab the metal picks into the ice. Yes! It grabs hold. Suddenly I feel like I have a chance.

"Just short, choppy strokes," Dworkin advises me. "And then, once you're out, you need to roll away from the hole."

I stab the ice again, this time a little farther from the hole. Then again. And again. Short, choppy strokes. Now I have a good grip on the edge of the ice, and I pull myself out of the hole, rolling over onto my side, then rolling over a few times, feeling a bit like a slug. This might not look like what an action hero would do, but the rolling is important.

"Roll away, because we're distributing our weight across the ice," explains Dworkin.

In other words, if you stood up, you might crack the ice again and you're back to square one. I keep rolling and make it to solid ground. "Good job!" says Dworkin.

Okay, but what happens if your friend or relative falls in? Again I drop myself into the freezing water, again gritting my teeth, again—almost literally—freezing my ass off. Dworkin plays the role of friend or relative. For a second I wait for him to race toward me and pull me out . . . but he doesn't.

SURVIVAL TIP 3: Stay onshore and try a rescue from there.

Don't rush in to rescue them. That's human nature, but that could also get *both* of you killed. Instead, stay on solid ground and use a rope, a tree branch, jumper cables, or anything that can work as a lifeline.

"Tell the victim to wrap it around his wrist, and we can help pull him out," explains Dworkin. This way no one else is put in danger, and you have an even higher chance of saving the victim.

He tosses me a rope. I catch it, still freezing, and pull myself out of the deadly watery hole. Again I roll away toward solid ground and safety.

Phew. I feel my heartbeat return to normal. *Let's not do that again.*

. . . Your Parasail Snaps

There are very few things that I refused to do for Rossen Reports. But the one thing I wouldn't do is parasail, thanks to a crippling fear of heights. So what does any self-respecting journalist do? That's right, I send my producers straight into the heart of danger, risking their lives instead of mine. (Thanks, Josh and Lindsey!)

Floating over the ocean looks tranquil and beautiful and soul-enriching, and it can be, but it can also turn deadly. The National Transportation Safety Board (NTSB) has deemed parasailing "risky," after more and more accidents suggest a breakdown in safety protocols. In one tragedy, a six-year-old boy was floating in the air—having the ride of his life—until a gust of wind slammed him into the wall of a hotel. (Incredibly, he survived.) In another, two teenage girls were joyfully sailing through the sky . . . until a rope snapped and they crashed into a tall building, then fell from the sky and smashed onto the roof of a car. They were seriously injured.

Just how safe is it? I bravely ask Josh and Lindsey to find out. We start in Florida, posing as undercover tourists, and I send Josh and Lindsey up high in the sky, waving at them from below.

"Wow, this is so cool!" Josh shouts, a huge smile on his face, very careful to keep his journalistic objectivity.

"This is craazzaaaay!" Lindsey smiles and waves.

They have a blast and I stay safely on the boat—everyone wins. And in Florida, in fact, the parasailing companies—at least the ones we try—*do* indeed have safety regulations, and the procedures are indeed being followed.

Then we head to Cancún. (This job requires certain sacrifices.) When Josh and Lindsey get to their first boat, they're launched into the air *without any safety briefing whatsoever*—not a word.

High in the air, Josh looks at Lindsey and says, "He didn't ask a thing."

"Barely even spoke to us," says Lindsey, amazed.

They're now sailing high above me in the sky, way *too* high. Experts say you should be no higher than 400 feet. They are way higher than that. Josh looks at Lindsey, concerned. "Let's see what they would do if we were to start screaming."

She nods.

"Heeyyyy!" yells Josh.

They can't hear him.

"Let us down!" yells Lindsey.

Nothing.

"Hey, we want to come down!" Josh yells from high above.

I couldn't hear them either—I only saw their panicked screams later, when watching the footage we shot in the sky. If there was a problem? A gust of wind? They'd be goners.

After they safely land (thank God) I have some questions for the operator. "Jeff Rossen from NBC News," I say, shaking his hand. "Do you think you should have given a safety briefing?"

The operator considers this. It's almost like I had asked him a nonsensical question, like, *Do you think you should have given them cherry lollypops?* The guy then says, as an excuse, "But they weren't looking that nervous."

"They didn't look nervous, so you didn't give them a briefing?"

"No."

That's unacceptable according to Mark McCulloh, a parasailing safety expert, who was watching everything from the beach. "If you're on the boat and the operator does not give you a safety briefing, you need to leave that boat right away," he explains.

Yet this is nothing compared to our next Cancún operator. (Somehow, even after that experience, Josh and Lindsey have the guts to go back in the air.) On the next boat, the actual harnesses themselves—the things strapping your body to the sail—have worn down, frayed edges. One is on the verge of coming apart. There are tears every-where. I could easily rip it in two. I tell Josh to go up in the air with the frayed harness and we'll see what happens. *Kidding.* The operator claims that they don't use the frayed harness, but still, it's unsettling.

A little less enthusiastically than before, Josh and Lindsey soar into the air. They start out over the clear blue sea . . . but then they drift closer to the Cancún beach and the hotels. In fact, they get very close. Too close. They're almost swaying over the beach. What would happen if they hit a gust of wind? If the force is strong enough, they could slam into the high-rise hotels.

"Look how close we are to this hotel," Josh says to Lindsey, high up in the air. That joyful grin is long gone. "It's frightening."

"I mean, we're practically over the beach right now," says Lind-sey with a note of panic.

Far below, in the boat, I have an even scarier view, as I have a front-row seat to the boat's "safety staff" that's responsible for the lives of my friends. One guy is texting on his phone. One guy en-joys a glass of water, staring into his cup, oblivious to my friends hurtling through the air. Sometimes they chat with each other. They rarely look up in the sky.

When Josh and Lindsey safely land (a minor miracle), it's time to reveal ourselves. I try to control my anger. "You guys were talk-ing. He was texting. Who was watching [my friends]?"

"The captain is the boss," says one of the crew.

Yet the "captain" was barely looking up, constantly checking his phone. What e-mail could be more important than the lives of his passengers? I don't care if he unlocked a new level in Pokémon Go. "He was on his phone, too," I say.

"We have experience," the crew member says. "We hear the

motor. We hear everything the captain is saying. Don't need to watch."

Don't need to watch? Mark McCulloh, our parasailing safety expert, is shocked. "Watching that ride was the most frightening thing I've seen in my career," he tells us. "If the rope had broke, or the engine had stalled, they would have flown right into the buildings. They could have died."

So does this mean that you should never go parasailing? No one's saying that. But if you decide to risk it, make sure you get a safety briefing, make sure you check the harness, and make sure the ropes look up to snuff.

There is one bit of good news—after our report, that last scary company changed its policy and banned its employees from using phones; they can't even bring them on the boat. Progress. Let's hope more companies do the same. And Josh, Lindsey? All kidding aside—I owe you.

. . . Your Concert Tickets Are Fake

I'm old enough to remember a time when if you tried to buy concert tickets "online," your friends would squint their eyes at you and say something like, "Are you a *freak?* You bought your tickets *online?*" Back then, buying concert tickets *online* seemed as crazy as, say, buying *books* online, or maybe "live streaming" a movie on your computer. This was sometime between 1890 and 2000.

Now, everyone does it. In fact, it's almost impossible to buy tickets *offline.* Yet paradoxically, somehow, it can seem harder to buy tickets online than ever before. Tickets to see a hot artist go on sale and then, minutes later, they vanish. Does it sometimes seem like no matter how many times you click Refresh, no matter how long you wait, and no matter how perfectly you time your purchase, you have *no chance* at scoring the tickets?

You're right.

"It's a fixed game," says New York Attorney General Eric Schneiderman, who sat down with me in 2016 to explain the issue. "Ordinary ticket purchasers really don't have a fair shot at tickets to most shows."

Schneiderman had issued a report saying this extends beyond just music concerts, but also theater and sporting events—basically any big show. Just how bad is this?

"We determined that, on average, 54 percent of the tickets never even make it to the vendors who sell to the public," says the attorney general.

That sort of blows my mind. *The majority* of tickets don't even go to regular folks like you and me. So where the hell *do* they go? I reached out to a man who would know, Jon Potter, the president of a fans' rights group (there's a group for everything), funded by StubHub.

"Who's getting them?" I ask Potter.

"They're giving them to the high-end credit-card holders who get the e-mail three days before you ever knew the concert was going on sale," says Potter. "They're giving them to the fan club, and then many of them go to the artist, or to the venue."

And the numbers are staggering. For a One Direction show in New Jersey, for example, box-office records show that at least 64 percent of tickets were held back or sold to special groups. Or take Justin Bieber. At a concert in Fresno, *92 percent* of tickets went to special groups or were held back entirely. Translation? Of the more than 12,000 seats, only 940 were set aside for the official sale date.

One Direction wouldn't comment and we didn't hear back from Justin Bieber. But Ticketmaster told us it "fully cooperated with the attorney general's office . . ." and will continue ". . . to ensure that artists can get tickets into the hands of their fans."

There's yet another problem. The attorney general is also going after ticket brokers who use software called "bots," where, basically, these little robots can gobble up hundreds of tickets in seconds, then resell them online for a *lot* more money. For one U2 concert, these robots scooped up more than one thousand tickets in the first minute of sale.

But let's pretend that you somehow bought tickets. You saved up the money, you agreed to pay the king's ransom for a One Direction or Taylor Swift concert, and maybe you bought the tickets for your kids. This was the case of fifteen-year-old cousins Chloe and Hailee, who wanted one thing more than anything in the world: to see a Taylor Swift concert.

Hailee's mom saved up all year. She told the girls that if they got good grades, they could go to the concert. The girls studied. The girls did their homework. And the girls made the honor roll. *Taylor Swiiiiiffffttt!!!!!*

Hailee's mom went online to buy tickets—sold out. But she had *promised* the girls she would take them to see Taylor Swift—and the girls made the honor roll—so she was determined. She would find a way. She went online and bought tickets from a third-party broker, shelling out nearly a thousand bucks.

The girls couldn't wait.

"We waited about the whole entire year for this to happen, and even had a countdown on our phone," Hailee tells me.

"It was that big of a deal for you?"

"It was a very big deal."

The big day finally came. Hailee's mom took the girls to the concert, and they showed up at the gate, presenting printouts of their tickets.

They were turned away. The girls burst into tears, their teenage dreams turning to ashes.

The tickets were fake. It turns out this happens all the time. Just like with counterfeit prom dresses (see page 79), these con artists are *good*. They might be evil but they are not stupid. These aren't a bunch of teenagers mocking up tickets using Photoshop; these are well-oiled machines, actual businesses, and you would never know from the website that they aren't.

To test this out, my producer Jovanna goes online to purchase tickets for an Ariana Grande concert, and the tickets sure do look legit. Real photos, real seat numbers, real details on the tickets. But she calls Ticketmaster to see if the tickets are real or not—and they're fake.

Huh. Let's see what happens. . . . She reaches out to the seller and says she wants to buy the tickets. We set up a meet.

It feels a little cloak-and-dagger, literally meeting up with this stranger to exchange tickets for cash. (I really should have worn a trench coat.)

"You swear these aren't fake?" Jovanna asks the seller.

"I swear to God."

"It's two hundred dollars, right?"

"Yeah."

"All right, thank you," Jovanna says, paying the man.

"Enjoy," says the seller of these fake tickets. "Thanks so much."

Now I reveal myself. "Hi, Jeff Rossen, with NBC News. Can we get our money back? Those tickets are fake."

The seller then *darts* across the street, as if he's a fugitive on the run, and in a sense, he is. I think about chasing him but remember that I'm not a cop or a very fast runner. Now, just like Hailee and Chloe, we're out some serious money and stuck with . . . nothing.

And as for Hailee and Chloe? They had the worst experience, where you actually get to the concert, look forward to it all day—or *all year*, in their case—and then get turned away. The kids are devastated. The parents are crushed, because we feel like *we let our children down*. You flip from Father of the Year to Worst Dad Ever. I'll be honest. As a guy who's on the road and travels three to four days a week, I look forward to special occasions like this. It's a way to surprise and delight my kids and to show them that I love them. So if this gift backfires? It's heartbreaking.

Two more things. First, when you buy the tickets, use a credit card so that you can later dispute the charge. And only buy tickets from verified sites—if it looks too good to be true . . .

Second: We later caught up with Hailee and Chloe. "We know how hard you worked to earn those concert tickets," I say to Hailee.

She nods.

"And even though the tour is sold out . . . we called in a favor."

What the girls didn't know? We got four tickets for a Taylor Swift show in Florida, and we flew the family down to see her. Great seats. The girls cried again . . . this time with joy.

TICKETMASTER'S ADVICE ON HOW TO AVOID BUYING FAKES

If you can, buy your tickets from official sources. Examples include the box office, the primary ticketer (such as Ticketmaster), and official outlets like LiveNation.com and NBATickets.com. This is the safest option.

But if you're buying from secondary ticketing websites, make sure you're dealing with a reputable business. Here are some things to check:

1. Transaction terms should be stated up front. Know how much you're being charged up front, before you purchase.

2. Make sure they state their refund policy.

3. Look for identification showing that they're a reseller. The website should state that the tickets are being resold.

4. Check for specifics on the actual tickets, which include shipping terms and availability dates.

. . . You Realize: "I'm Drunk"

Let's be honest. For most adults, "fun and games" means having a few drinks. And *no one* ever sets out to drink and drive. No one wakes up in the morning, eats a bowl of cereal, has some coffee, and says to themselves, "Tonight I'm going to have a bunch of booze, and then I will drive home." And yet, according to the National Highway Traffic Safety Administration, nearly 10,000 Americans are killed from alcohol-related crashes; it accounts for roughly one in three highway deaths. So how does this math work? How come *no one* thinks they will drink and drive, yet somehow it's killing thousands?

To help understand the problem, I conduct an experiment where I . . . well, I guess I throw the worst party in the world. I host a big shindig that offers plenty of free drinks. (I'm their hero!) But what my guests don't know is that I also invited a cop, with a Breathalyzer. I even keep track of how much each guest drinks. (I'm their enemy!) It's the ultimate party foul—bringing a cop to the party. And not a "hot cop" who has stripper pants that tear away with Velcro; this is an actual cop who could put people in jail.

PRO TIP: Never invite me to your party.

In fairness, the group wasn't *totally* blindsided, as we told them that we were doing a story on drinking habits. (Partly true.) We tell them to drink normally. We pour all the booze they want. Everyone has a great time. We serve martinis, wine, beer, mixed drinks. Some people do shots. (Don't worry, we have designated drivers and car services to take everyone home safely.)

As the boozy party begins to wind down, I pull about a dozen drinkers into one room. I look at them all. Men and women in their twenties and thirties and forties. No one looks plastered. "Show of hands," I say to the group. "How many of you feel in control of yourselves?"

Nearly everyone raises their hands.

I ask one woman if she's okay to drive home right now.

She shakes her head. "I'd wait longer."

"How long would you wait before you drove?"

She pauses, considering. "Maybe—at least an hour, hour and a half."

So we call her bluff. An hour later we speak to the woman again, and this time we happen to have a Breathalyzer. (She must have been so thrilled!) The legal limit is a 0.08 blood alcohol content. The lady blows into the Breathalyzer . . . and comes back with a 0.10.

She's stunned. "I thought I could have two [drinks] and be safe."

Most people have that kind of assumption. I know I do. But authorities say that even *after* you stop drinking, your blood alcohol level can actually continue to *rise* as liquor seeps into your system.

Or take another partier, a good-natured guy named Art, who stopped drinking a full *two hours* earlier. We give him the Breathalyzer . . . and he blows a 0.12. Well over the legal limit.

Most of the drinkers tell us that they would *not* drive home—keep in mind they had cameras pointing at their faces, so, frankly, I'm not sure I totally buy that—but one of the partiers, Ron, admits that he *would* drive home in his condition. He says that if he lived close by a local bar, then yeah, sure, he could safely drive home.

"Two blocks, I'm good," Ron says confidently.

"You think you could do it safely?" I ask.

"Two blocks, yeah."

Enter the police officer.

Our cop gives Ron a field-sobriety test, asking him to walk slowly in a straight line, heel to toe. Ron takes one step, two, three, four—so far, so good—and then, on step five, his body twists like a pretzel. Ron looks shocked, his world turned upside down. So we give him a Breathalyzer. Ron blows into the Breathalyzer, the cop stares at the machine, waits a moment, and then says, "Zero point one three."

"Zero point one three?" Ron asks, not quite believing it.

"Zero point one three. You're legally intoxicated."

"Wow," Ron says. "Three drinks and I'm intoxicated?"

Actually, it turns out that he did *not* just have three drinks. That was the other part of the experiment. We kept track of each and every beverage—once again, I'm the life of the party—and we compared what people *thought* they drank to what they *actually* drank. It turns out that our brain plays tricks. Ron did not have three drinks. He had five drinks—four martinis and a shot. We tell ourselves narratives like *I'm a good driver, I'm responsible, I won't drink and drive* and then, to fit that narrative, our brain sort of fudges the details.

Put differently, our brain thinks that *Maybe it doesn't count as "drinking and driving" if we're barely "drinking," right? And surely just two or three drinks doesn't really count as DRINKING, right?* Wrong.

There's a misperception that people feel they can go out and have a few drinks when, in reality, *one drink* can impair you. And for many, two drinks is enough to count as legally intoxicated, get you tossed in jail, or cause you to get in a crash and do the unthinkable.

Ron still looks shaken. "It's disheartening," he says, looking at the ground.

"That you would have gotten on the road," I say.

"Yeah. Very scary."

"What do you make of that now?"

"I'm an idiot. And you don't realize how much you've drunk until after the sobriety test comes."

"And by then it's too late."

"And then it's absolutely too late. God forbid, I'd hurt somebody or, you know, killed somebody," says Ron.

Ron has the guts to face the truth. And he says he'll change. Let's all follow his lead.

. . . You're Buried Alive

This one touches all of us at NBC. A colleague was working on Mt. Everest, filming a show, and trekking up the snow-capped mountains. An avalanche came from nowhere. It killed someone in his own tent. Our colleague was shaken and so were we.

Even if you're not an Everest thrill seeker or a mountain climber or a skier, odds are you know someone who is. And the odds get scary pretty quick. Every year, avalanches kill more than 150 people and injure thousands more, they appear without warning and, if you're not prepared, they can bury you alive.

So how do you survive an avalanche? I trekked to the slopes of Park City, Utah, to get a crash course from Sue Anderson, an expert from Wasatch Backcountry Rescue. It's freezing on the mountains. I bundle up in a ski jacket and try to keep warm, rubbing my hands together.

"The first thing you want to do is stay on top," Anderson instructs me. I know she must be cold but she hides it better than I do, wearing a red ski jacket and a red knit cap. She waves her arms in the air as if she's swimming, doing a backstroke, and I try to mimic her. The idea is that if an avalanche is coming at you, the goal is to use your arms and legs and summon all your strength to *stay on top* of the flying snow and debris. If possible, try to go *with* the direction of the avalanche, so if it's going to the left, you go left.

"What if it comes on top of me and I'm *not* on top?" I ask.

"If it buries over your face, you want to fight," Anderson says, and she punches her fists in the air. "You want to swing. You want to punch. You want to fight as hard as you can to try to stay on top of that snow." Again she punches the air, quickly, with rapid strokes, like Rocky working the speed bags. I try to imitate her.

Here's why "staying on top" is so important: Don't be fooled by the fluffiness of snow. After an avalanche, it immediately turns hard as concrete, burying you alive. You have only seconds before that happens. Those seconds are critical. I'm not talking thirty seconds or twenty seconds, I'm talking five seconds or less.

When stuck in an avalanche, your best chance of survival is to *punch for an airway.* Even if you're not able to completely dig yourself out of the snow, punching an airway will make you far, far less likely to suffocate.

What if you get trapped? It turns out that your clothes can save you. (Who said fashion was frivolous?) Many popular brands of ski pants and jackets have a little tracking device, called the Recco, that's smaller than a pack of gum. It's sewn into the jacket itself.

"How long does this last?" I ask, holding up the tiny gadget.

"It never dies."

"This *never* dies?"

"Nope, that's the beauty of it," she says. (Finally. Some good news.)

To put the Recco in action, we conduct a little experiment where they bury me alive. (By now, you knew that was coming, right?) We don't tell Sue Anderson the location of my burial. But I'm hoping she can find me from the signal tracker in my Recco. Wearing my Recco-enabled ski jacket, I climb into a tiny cave that's basically the size of, well, a coffin. If you're in this situation, it will be dark. It will be cold. And I'm insanely claustrophobic. They seal the cave and now I'm all alone. Cue Simon & Garfunkel singing "Hello darkness, my old friend . . ."

Did I mention it's dark? You've never seen true blackness until you've been buried alive. Even at home when your lights are out, there's still that faint electronic glow from the digital clock on your cable box. Here? Nothing. And it's bone-chilling cold, yet somehow I'm sweating and I also feel hot, almost feverish. Now I understand why "being buried alive" is near the very top of most people's fears. Did I mention I'm beyond claustrophobic?

Yet I tell myself one thing: *Breathe.* Breathe calmly. Breathe slowly. Experts say that if you are buried, the key to survival is to control your breathing. It could mean the difference between lasting a few minutes or a few days. Oxygen is now my most precious resource, and I need to use it wisely. Breathe in. Breathe out. It's so dark. It's so cold. *Help.*

Meanwhile, Sue Anderson is skiing back and forth on the mountain, holding a little meter that beeps louder and faster as she gets closer. The beeps fade when she gets farther away.

Finally I hear the sound of distant shouting. Sue Anderson. "Helllllo?"

I yell out a response, trying to avoid sounding panicked.

"Hey, is anyone in there?" Anderson calls out.

"I am!"

"We're going to get you out of here!" Anderson says.

And, of course, she did. My ski jacket's homing beacon guided her toward me, exactly as intended. Even though my life was never *really* in danger, it sure felt like it was, and that's another reminder of how terrifying *actual* life-and-death experiences must be. So the more you know beforehand, the better.

. . . Your Carnival Game Is Rigged

It happens like clockwork. I'll be on a boardwalk or at a carnival with my family, we'll walk by one of those games where you spray a water gun at a target, and my kids will see a giant teddy bear.

"Daddy, can we play that?" my son Blake will say.

"Dad, can you win me a teddy bear?" my daughter Sloane will ask, opening her seven-year-old eyes so wide that it's impossible to resist.

And my ten-year-old, Skyler, piles on, "C'mon, Daddy!"

"It's easy!" the carnival worker will say, and then he'll demonstrate how simple it is to spray the water gun. So easy! How could you even miss? These carny workers are evil geniuses. In fact they are *brilliant.* They always go for the child, knowing that once your kid is on the hook, *you* are on the hook. So of course I'll cave, we'll play the stupid game, and twenty dollars later we fail to win a giant teddy bear, but instead a goldfish that my daughter wants to name Tie-Dye. It sure *feels* like the games are rigged. Just what, exactly, are their secrets?

To find the wizard behind the curtain, I seek the advice of Rich Margittay, a retired police officer, who has spent thirty-five years investigating rigged carnival games. He set up a carnival to show me.

Our first stop is the basketball hoop, which Rich calls "a classic," a game that's at nearly every boardwalk and carnival.

I grab a basketball and take a shot—*swish.* "Boom!" I say, pretty pleased with myself.

"Excellent," says Rich. "Why don't you try this one?"

He directs me to a second hoop. It looks the same as the first.

I shoot. Clank. Big miss.

Rich then does a side-by-side comparison of the two hoops. The first one has a round rim, similar to the ones they use in regulation basketball. The second?

"It's oval. It's only 17 by 10.5 inches. The ball barely fits," explains Rich. That's the one many carnivals use. It's oval! And the next time you're at the carnival, notice how they line the sides with hanging teddy bears so you can't get a great view of the hoop. Just the view from the front, where it *looks* round.

So even if Steph Curry himself were to shoot the absolute perfect jump shot, the ball would barely fit through this hoop. "Plus, we have a little Inflategate here," says Rich, showing me the ball. Sure enough, the ball is overinflated—massively overinflated—so it's even more likely to bounce out.

Next, we visit a game called "tubs o' fun!" It looks easy enough; you just throw a ball into a large tub. How hard can it be? (Plus, "tubs o' fun!" is an all-time great name. It's almost worth a dollar just to hear someone say those words.)

"I'll play the carny and you can play the customer," Rich tells me. "You get two free shots and see how easy it is to win." This is the trick—convincing me I can't lose.

I toss the first ball into the tub—easy.

I toss the second ball—easy. These really are tubs o' fun!

"Jeff, I just cheated you," Rich says, in something of a buzzkill. He points to the bottom of the tub. "There was a third ball in here. The third ball cuts down on the bounciness, [so when your balls go in,] they stay in. But when you play for the money, there is no 'deadening' ball inside there. You have to throw with no help." That's right, the carny quietly takes that third ball out when your money comes out.

I try it again, this time without the "deadening ball" at the bottom. My ball bounces out.

"And you lose," says Rich.

Suddenly the tubs aren't as fun.

We then head to our last game, a contest so impossible to win that even the *FBI* investigated it: the ring toss.

"With this one, Jeff, they let you come in really close," Rich tells me. We inch superclose to the target—a glass bottle, and the goal is to toss a ring around this bottle. We get to within arm's length of this bottle—you can practically touch it. It looks almost comically easy; how could anyone possibly miss from this distance?

"And they give you all these rings," Rich says.

So many chances to win! So close to the target! It's impossible to lose.

I toss a ring—nope. A second—nope.

"Come on, come on!" I yell in frustration.

"You're gonna lose," says Rich.

"What's happening here?" I ask, deflated.

The problem, he explains, is that "the rings barely fit over the neck of the bottle."

I inspect it closer. Sure enough, even if I hold the bottle in my hand and carefully put the ring around it—at a perfect angle—the ring just barely fits.

"You can't win this," I say.

"It's gambling and it's wrong," Rich agrees. "Carnivals are making lots of money off the backs of children. And that needs to stop."

When we reached out, the Outdoor Amusement Business Association told me that many states regulate games, and most games have to be winnable. They said state law-enforcement officials come out to verify they are games of skill.

Not *all* carnival games are rigged, of course. But if you're worried, experts say to play the games where you compete against other players, as there's always a winner. (This is sort of like how smart and experienced gamblers might choose to play poker over something like blackjack.)

BONUS TIP: If you're playing the balloon dart game, pay attention to how inflated the balloons are.

At many carnivals, they will actually let the balloons deflate, making them harder to pop. Aim for the balloons with the most air.

Okay, but honestly? At the end of the day, in a sense, none of that really matters. Maybe the game is rigged, but of course I'll go back to play it. The kids will drag me back again and again, and I, a weak man, am powerless to resist. We've won goldfish after goldfish, even though they never survive for very long.

R.I.P., Tie-Dye.

5

PROTECTING YOUR KIDS

I'M A PARENT. SO, FOR me, this is as serious as it gets. We do everything we can to keep our kids safe, but sometimes there are hidden dangers that not even the most savvy parents know about. These tips can save lives and, in the case of train-track photos, they may have already saved mine. . . .

- ⊚ Confession: I Put My Kids in Danger
- ⊚ You're Buckling Your Kids All Wrong
- ⊚ Your Little Angel Is a Cheater
- ⊚ Sleeping Through a Fire Emergency
- ⊚ Fighting Identity Thieves Who Target You and Your Baby
- ⊚ Breaking into Hot Cars
- ⊚ My School Security Test Should Scare the Hell Out of You
- ⊚ The Safest School in America
- ⊚ The Claw Machine Hates My Son

Confession: I Put My Kids in Danger

I like to take my kids to the train tracks. Maybe this hearkens back to my own childhood, when my dad took me to the tracks and I was mesmerized by the wooden planks, the iron bolts, and the steel lines that seemed to stretch from my feet to infinity. There's a certain romance to trains. Unlike computers or the Internet or electrical cables, trains are something concrete, visible, that we can imagine connecting all of America.

I've always loved trains, my son loves trains, my daughters love—well, okay, my daughters can take them or leave them—but my son really, really loves trains. So we would often go to the train tracks, I would check the schedule to make sure no trains were coming, I would look in both directions to ensure the coast was clear, and then, when it was perfectly safe, we would stand on the tracks and snap some photos.

My dad and I did this when I was a kid, and somehow this made me feel connected to him, passing it down to the next generation. A great way for my kids to truly *feel* the magic of trains, as they would touch the wooden planks and I'd explain how a train works. Of course I remained aware of my surroundings, ready to scurry the kids off the tracks if I heard the distant rumbling of a locomotive.

I was actually proud of it, helping to teach my kids about the wonder of trains. So in an unrelated Rossen Reports segment, one of the photos I showed on TV was one of my kids standing on the tracks. But then I got a big surprise: a barrage of angry e-mails from viewers.

"You are a horrible parent."

Another: "You're the worst parent on earth."

Another cheery note: "YOU'RE PUTTING YOUR KIDS IN DANGER."

More: "Trains kill people on tracks. What's wrong with you?"

And this one: "Don't you watch the news?"

Wait, what the hell was going on? I don't have any illusions that I'm the World's Best Dad—coffee mug or no—but I didn't think I was the absolute *worst* dad, either. Yet somehow I had become Public Enemy #1.

Again, for context, I had checked the train schedule—*all clear!*—and I listened carefully for the sound of approaching trains, ensuring that my kids were not at risk. But the e-mails, tweets, and Facebook messages kept flooding in.

"How dare you say you're an expert!"

"I HATE YOU, JEFF ROSSEN."

I did more research, and sure enough, the outraged viewers were right: Trains were killing people and, specifically, they were killing people who posed for selfies and group photos. But how was that even possible? To be honest, part of me wondered, *Were those people just not paying attention?* I mean, it's a freaking *train*, right? And trains are loud. When a train roars past me it's usually too loud to talk; I have to cover my ears. It seems impossible for a train to "sneak up" on me.

Yet the statistics don't lie. In 2015 alone, more than 300 people were killed trespassing on train tracks, many of them posing for photos and all of them, like me, were convinced that they could hear the train coming. Prom photos, wedding photos, family photos. Some of the pictures are haunting. In one, three teenage girls pose for a selfie, smiling at the camera, and in the background, just above the girls' heads, you can see the oncoming train. Seconds later they were killed.

"Trains are very large, so people think that they're very loud," explains Libby Rector Snipe, a train safety expert with Operation Lifesaver. "The truth is, they're relatively quiet. If an engineer sees someone on the tracks, even if they apply the emergency break, it takes them a mile or more for them to stop."

But still . . . I was skeptical. I mean it's a *train*. Have you ever seen a silent train? I sure haven't. I still didn't totally get the danger.

So we set up an experiment. CSX Transportation gives us special access to a stretch of their train tracks, and they arrange a crew standing by to ensure I stay safe. Then, when standing just to the side of the tracks, I turn my back to an oncoming train. I wonder . . . how close would the train get before I could hear it?

When the train is far in the distance, I hear nothing. When it comes closer, I hear nothing. When it's clearly visible to anyone standing next to me, I hear nothing. It is only *seconds* before it would have splattered me that I hear the train. *Good God.* Maybe I would have time to jump out of the way, maybe not. What if my son tripped and fell? What if my daughter stepped on a shoelace when trying to run off the tracks in time? Now, finally, I understood all those angry tweets and e-mails. And the train in our experiment was only going 25 miles per hour; some trains hit speeds of 70, 80, even 90 miles per hour. My children could have been killed.

One thing I didn't realize is that most trains today are not, in fact, like the chugging locomotives from 1898. My son likes to say *Chugga chugga chooo chooo!!* when playing with his toy trains, but they don't really work like that anymore. They're electric, efficient, silent. Yes, it's true that trains are still loud when they rumble right by you, but that roaring sound only occurs *after* the train has reached you—not before. Believe it or not, trains are silent in front and only loud in the back as the wheels clack over the tracks. You don't hear that in front, only as it's going by.

My goal with Rossen Reports is to help people be safer, act smarter and, in my heart of hearts, I hope that I'm helping people save lives. Yet this time the script was flipped. You saved *my* life. Thank you.

You're Buckling Your Kids All Wrong

A buddy of mine is a police officer. He once told me, "Oh, I see it all the time. Parents drive their kids to school, but the kids aren't buckled up."

I didn't believe the guy. Every parent knows that their kids should wear seat belts, right? That's Mom & Dad 101. It's as basic as it gets. "Make your kid wear a seat belt" is about as complicated as "Feed your kid food."

Yet car crashes are the leading cause of death for children, and police say that in many of these cases, the kids aren't wearing their seat belts. Just how widespread is the problem? The Broward Sheriff's Department of Fire Rescue in Florida has a policy of pulling over cars to do random spot-checks. I tagged along one day to see for myself. (This is the closest I would ever get to being an actual sheriff's deputy. Sadly, they didn't give me a gun or handcuffs.)

We pull over one car—a mom with her adorable son happily sitting in the backseat . . . without a seat belt.

"Why wasn't your son in the seat belt?" I ask.

"Oh, I just forgot," says the mom.

"You just forgot?"

"Yeah."

We pull over another car—same thing. Car after car, minivan after minivan.

"I forgot," says another.

"I forgot," says a third.

"I *told* them to belt in," one mother tells me, but then she never checked to make sure he actually did it. In the end, a full 50 percent of the cars had kids without seat belts. Incredible. It's even more alarming when you consider what happens with crash tests—shown on those videos where a dummy goes flying through the windshield. These tests show that the dummy could easily get killed . . . even at speeds of just thirty miles per hour. Many of us think "I'm only going a few blocks" or "I'm not going very fast." But the truth is that *even at very slow speeds*, and even in just a few short blocks, without a seat belt, the child could die. It happens all the time.

And there's an even sneakier problem. Some parents *do* make sure their kid is buckled and, in the winter, like a good parent, they send their kid to school with a heavy coat. This is what responsible parents do, right? You give your kid a coat so they don't freeze. That's what I do with my kids.

Yet was I doing it wrong?

"I think you are," says Sue Auriemma, a safety expert at Kids and Cars. "Show me what you do."

I invited Sue to watch me buckle up my son, Blake. So I do what I always do: I first zip up his big puffy jacket, plop him in the car seat, and then securely fasten the seat belt. Good to go.

"This feels snug to me," I say, tugging the straps a bit.

"It *looks* like it's tight," says Sue, nodding. "But it's actually loose. Let's take him out and take the jacket off."

I remove Blake's jacket. I stick him back in the car seat, and then I buckle the belt. *Whoa.* Without all that padding from the jacket, the seat belt is loose. It's extremely loose. I can easily fit my hand between the belt and Blake's chest. The belt flaps and flops around. The winter coat is filled with air, so in an accident, it immediately crushes down.

"This is unreal," I say.

"Isn't it? It's actually dangerous," says Sue.

Truth be told, I still didn't fully believe it. So, I visit a crash lab, where they test this very issue in Michigan. The engineers have set up a fake car that crashes into a wall, and they ask me to strap a child-size crash-test dummy into a car seat *without* a winter coat. I do so. I watch as the car whooshes forward at thirty miles per hour, then smashes into a wall. The crash-test dummy is fine—it just jostles forward a few inches.

Now let's see what happens when the dummy is wearing a winter coat. I zip up the puffy coat on the crash-test dummy, working from muscle memory, as this is what I do every winter morning for my own children. Then I snugly fasten the seat belt.

Standing a safe distance away, I watch the car—with my (simulated) child in the backseat, wearing a winter coat—get to a speed of thirty miles per hour. Again, it smashes into a wall. This time the child flings forward, shoots out from the backseat, and then zooms into the windshield. In a real crash he would have shattered the glass and likely been killed. The only thing the seat belt protected, ironically, was the puffy winter coat, which remained safely in the car seat, swaying back and forth.

That could have been Sloane. That could have been Blake. Or Skyler. That could have been your child.

A little shaken, I ask the woman who runs the lab, Miriam Manary, what parents should do to protect their kids. The first thing: Take *off* the winter coat.

"We want to see a nice tight fit of the harness to the child's body," says Miriam. "You should not be able to pinch any webbing up at the shoulder. And the harness clip should be at armpit level." And if they get cold? You can put the winter coat on *over* the seat belt, or just give them a blanket.

This tip might just save my own kids' lives. I hope others can learn, too.

Your Little Angel Is a Cheater

I've seen a lot of surprising statistics, but this one takes the cake: According to the International Center for Academic Integrity, 68 percent of college kids admit to cheating. That's 68 percent! More than half.

Cheating is easier than ever. As and Bs are just a few clicks away on the Internet, as clever kids have gamed the system. Like budding entrepreneurs, these cheaters have discovered a need in the market, and they swooped in to provide their services. It's Capitalism 101.

But what, exactly, does the cheating look like? How does it work? And *how easy* is it, really? To find out, we do a bit of cheating of our own: We pretend that a young *Today* show staffer, let's call her "Taylor," is an actual college student who needs help with a book report on Louisa May Alcott's classic, *Little Women*.

Taylor might be a fake student, but we actually use a real English professor, Bethany Schneider of Bryn Mawr College, to give a proper assignment—a "five- to six-page paper."

"A pretty straightforward English assignment," I clarify.

"Yes, absolutely."

Once she gets her assignment, Taylor takes her paperback copy of *Little Women* and tosses it aside. She won't be needing that! Instead of cracking open the book, she goes online and searches for "custom college papers." Within seconds she sees hundreds of postings. It's all right there in the open. No shame. We scroll through ads that promise "guaranteed grades" and quote the "price per page" almost as if we're using a website to buy an airline ticket, searching for the best deal.

Theoretically she could do it all online. But we wanted more info. Who *are* these mysterious people who write the papers? How much does it cost? Are the papers actually good?

We're about to find out. Taylor responds to two of the ads, hiring these faceless ghostwriters to pen her paper. She sets up meetings with each of them at a local diner.

First up is "Alex," who's maybe in his early twenties, and looks something like a young James Spader. He wears smart-guy glasses and a constant smirk. In his ad, Alex promises a "quick turnaround" and "years of experience."

"How are you?" Taylor asks, sliding into a booth.

"Good, how are you?" says Alex, as if this were a totally normal conversation, or maybe an awkward first date. Alex explains his process to reassure Taylor, clarifying that he writes the original papers himself, doesn't copy, and that, if necessary, he'll even learn new subjects to help out his clients. "I wrote, like, an entire final paper for someone's tech class about how to set up a network system," says Alex with another smirk, laughing a bit.

"Oh, my gosh!" says Taylor, pretending to be impressed.

"So that was a pain, because I had to teach myself how to do that and then write the paper on it." Alex charges $140. He clarifies that "I never guarantee an A, I usually guarantee people, like, a B."

Alex soon leaves the diner, presumably to start analyzing the lovely prose of Louisa May Alcott. Then Taylor meets with her second ghostwriter, Pete, who's a bit older and less cocky.

"Has any student ever gotten caught?" Taylor asks him.

"No."

"Never?"

Pete says that he does his own original writing. "So what I write, you cannot find online." Pete charges $90.

A week ticks by. The two ghostwriters study *Little Women* and separately compose their papers. Then Taylor sets up more meetings, ready to swap essays for cash. She pays them. They give her the papers.

When Pete leaves the diner, he gets a big surprise that he never could have predicted: me.

"Hi, Jeff Rossen, NBC News," I say to Pete.

"I've got to go," says Pete, in no mood to talk—especially with cameras rolling.

"This is your online ad," I say, and then I recite what Taylor saw online. " '*Party on the weekend, paper done Monday morning, get well above average grade guaranteed while you sleep through class.*' "

"Okay," says Pete.

"Isn't that pretty blatant?"

Quickly he changes strategies. "That's *not* me, actually."

"It *is* you," I say, incredulous. "We responded to the ad. Can you just stay and talk to us for a moment? We want to talk to you about the paper."

"I don't want to be on TV," says Pete, hiding his face with a notebook, and then he hustles away and ditches us, plunging into a subway entrance. See ya, Pete.

How about Alex, our young smirker? He had a very different reaction. As Alex leaves the diner, I approach him and introduce myself, half-expecting him to run away. "Hi, Alex. Jeff Rossen from NBC News."

The kid makes firm eye contact, smiles with confidence, and is happy to stay and chat.

"She gave you the book, you read it, you wrote the paper for her," I say, laying out the facts. "Isn't that cheating?"

Alex has a ready answer. "I mean, if she hands it in, that's her business." He tells me that when he sells students the papers, he explains that they should only be used as a "guide," not submitted to the teacher verbatim. Clever.

"Look, you're not breaking the law here," I concede. "But isn't this a question of ethics?"

He pauses. Considers. "I do [see] the ethical concern in it, but that's why I always advise people they have to make their own decisions."

"You make no apologies for this?"

"No."

Someday Alex will make an excellent lawyer.

Okay, so, ethics aside, were these papers any good? We have our professor read them both. She gives Alex a C minus; Pete gets a B. "So they pass?" I ask the professor.

"Yes, they pass."

"Would you have suspected either of these papers of cheating?"

"No."

"As a school official, what can you do to stop this?"

"I can teach my butt off and make my students want to write me an amazing paper."

So that's the world we live in. This cheating is tough to catch, hard to prevent, and maybe impossible to monitor. It happens all the time. And, when you think about it, maybe it's linked to other problems in the world. We talk about "gateway drugs," but this is a classic "gateway decision": When you get away with something small, next time you go bigger. When you take one shortcut in life, later you take a second, then a third. . . .

Sleeping Through
a Fire Emergency

When my daughter loses a tooth, that night I'll act as the Tooth Fairy and sneak into her room, hoping to leave her a small present. Yet no matter how quietly I tiptoe, somehow she has a knack for turning over and waking up at just the wrong moment. ("Daddy, is that you?") On other nights, she'll fall asleep watching the TV, so I gently turn off the screen and then, *boom!*, she has the uncanny ability to wake up.

It can seem like our kids wake up at the slightest of sounds. So it's only natural to assume that when it's really, really important—like when a smoke alarm sounds—our kids will hear the blaring siren. Besides, who can possibly sleep through *BEEP! BEEP! BEEP!*

But in a twist that's downright terrifying, experts say that, in many cases, children can sleep right through the alarm. I found this hard to believe, so I did what I always do when I'm skeptical: I set up an experiment.

Meet the Hollander family. In suburban Connecticut, the parents, Michelle and Josh, live with their three young boys—Duncan,

Hudson, and Sawyer. The kids have floppy hair and chase each other around the living room.

We tell the Hollanders that we're doing a story about sleeping and smoke detectors. Then we have a local fire captain, Captain Lynch, give the kids a fire-safety lesson.

"What would you do if you heard that sound in the middle of the night?" asks Captain Lynch.

"There would be smoke!" the youngest boy says.

"I would get up and I would get on the ground and crawl," another kid says.

They're both right. They know their stuff. But here's what we *didn't* tell the kids. We installed hidden infrared cameras in their bedrooms—we had permission from the parents, of course—and then a few days later, we came back in the middle of the night, working with their parents to see how they would react to a fire alarm.

"Good night," the mom says to the kids. She tucks them in and joins me downstairs.

"Will they wake up when that alarm sounds?" I ask the mom.

"I'm hoping they get up and, you know—"

"Know what to do?"

"Know what to do." She nods.

Along with the mom and dad, we watch the kids on a monitor downstairs. The Hollander boys are fast asleep.

The fire captain grabs a hockey stick, then uses it to tap the smoke alarm on the ceiling. It begins wailing: *BEEEEP! BEEEEEP! BEEEEP!!!*

The damn alarm hurts my ears—it is *loud*. Yet the boys keep sleeping. *BEEEEP! BEEEEEP! BEEEEP!* The boys are still fast asleep, cocooned under their blankets. Thirty seconds tick by. The boys remain asleep. A full minute. *BEEEEP! BEEEEEP! BEEEEP!* Then another minute.

Experts say that in a real emergency, their chances of survival would be slipping away.

"This could be a real fire right now," I say to the mom.

"And they would sleep right through it," she says. "It's so scary. . . ."

It has now been *three full minutes.* My thoughts race to my own kids, imagining Sloane, Blake, and Skyler sleeping through this blaring sound.

Finally we wake up the boys. "Did you hear that fire alarm going off?" I ask.

"No," says one.

"Didn't hear it at all?"

"No," says another.

This is no isolated incident. It's not a goofy outlier. According to a researcher at Ohio's Nationwide Children's Hospital, Dr. Gary Smith, this happens all the time. He has studied smoke detectors and sleeping children for years, and he tells me, "It would astound you at how loud the sounds can get, and the children continue to sleep through them."

"Why do kids sleep through these alarms?" I ask.

"They're simply not small adults, they're different biologically."

And that means they sleep differently?

"Children spend more time in *deep sleep* than adults do, and that's why it's harder for them to awaken in the case of an emergency," Dr. Smith says.

Given that biological difference, scientists are tackling the problem by trying to figure out what, exactly, will wake up the kids during a real fire. They're testing new things. In one proto-type, for example, parents can record their own voices in the alarm, telling the kids to wake up.

That might be years away, and it's still not a foolproof guarantee. In the meantime, there are things we can do right now, today, to help keep our kids safe. Captain Lynch says that when you create your fire-escape plan (see page 16), make sure that each adult is responsible for waking up a child. (So maybe it's Dad's job to wake up Timmy, Mom's job to wake up Suzie.)

And some real talk? I'll be even more blunt. After this experiment, now I know that in the event of a real fire at the Rossen home, as soon as I wake up, I'll be screaming my head off, making sure my kids are awake. Because every second counts.

Fighting Identity Thieves Who Target You and Your Baby

Meet Candida Guitierrez. She's a married kindergarten teacher who chased the American Dream—a good job, new home, the white picket fence.

Then she applied for a mortgage: *Denied*. This surprised her, as she was careful with her finances, so she asked the bank why they rejected her. They told her that it was her "house in Kansas."

Just two problems with this:

Problem 1: Candida lived in Texas, not Kansas.

Problem 2: Candida had never bought a home before.

But you know who did? A woman named Candida Guitierrez. It turns out that there *was* a Candida Guitierrez living in Kansas, and for years she had been using the same Social Security number, the same date of birth, the same everything. Investigators looked into the case and discovered that she was an ID thief, an impostor, who had stolen Candida's credentials to buy a house, get a job, and even get medical care for the birth of her two children . . . leaving the real Candida's credit in shambles.

The richest irony? In a truly audacious move, Not-Candida reached out to the Social Security Administration and claimed that *she* was the victim of identity theft, leaving Real-Candida even more in a lurch.

It's sobering, and experts say that this happens all the time. Theoretically, there could be someone out there living as Jeff Rossen, and they can get all the perks of my Social Security number, but without any of the chores of picking up the kids from school. (*Kidding*, Blake and Sloane and Skyler.)

So how do you protect yourself? The critical piece of information is the Social Security number. That's a thief's golden ticket. "Once an identity thief has our Social Security number and name, they can go out and get addresses, dates of birth, and then with that information, take out a driver's license, a credit card, open up a bank account," says Todd Feinman, the former CEO of Identity Finder. "And that's really when the worst type of identity fraud starts to occur."

This can go on for *years*—as in the case with Candida—and the longer it goes on, the longer the Not-Candidas can accumulate more evidence of *their* new identity.

But it gets worse. Far worse. These thieves might be evil but they are definitely not stupid, and they're now stealing the identities of *babies*. That's right. It's possible that my wife could give birth to a beautiful new daughter . . . who is already in debt.

My team tracked down a little toddler named Egan, an adorable two-year-old who happened to owe thousands in credit-card debt and has already declared bankruptcy.

"You think this must be a joke and then you realize, no, this is actually incredibly serious," Egan's mother tells us.

I meet a nine-year-old named Riley, who's already in default on utility bills. Her Social Security number was stolen eleven years before she was born.

There were more. Take Katie, who was only three years old when the crooks stole her identity. As a teenager, her credit report showed her over $750,000 in debt.

Are these just a few random outliers? Incredibly, our team discovers *thousands* of young victims nationwide. It turns out that the credentials of unborn babies are even more valuable than those of adults. "It's a blank check for these criminals," says Jamie May, vice president of operations for the security firm AllClear ID. "The child doesn't realize that they have a problem until they start using their credit."

So while your little kid learns how to walk and talk and ride a bike and then goes to kindergarten, some scumbag could be using her Social Security number to buy a new flat-screen TV.

"Never in my wildest dreams had I thought to run a credit check on my son," Egan's mom tells me. "And what parent would run a credit check on their child who's in diapers, who's crawling?"

Remember Katie, who was only three years old when her identity was stolen? "I think that because it is illegal, they should be in jail," she tells me.

But they're not. In perhaps the cruelest twist, often the authorities simply don't have the time or resources to track down the identity thieves . . . but in Katie's case, we did. With a little elbow grease, my team tracks down a guy named Manuel, who worked at an auto-repair shop just miles from Katie's house. I couldn't believe that he's just walking free, not behind bars, enjoying the same rights and privileges as you and me. I confront the guy.

"Have you been using a young girl's Social Security number?" I ask Manuel.

"I don't want to talk," he says.

We ask him if he took out nearly half a million dollars in loans using Katie's Social Security number, and asked him to explain himself.

He asks if I'm a police officer and if I'm arresting him.

"I'm not a police officer," I say. "I'm just trying to figure out why you did this."

He never gives me an answer.

It was so frustrating. We soon tracked down another identity thief, then another, and then another. Authorities know that a flaw in the credit system allows this charade. Here's the problem: When someone applies for, say, a loan, usually the bank only checks that the Social Security number has a good credit history. Believe it or not, most banks don't check whether that number was *assigned* to the name, because the government charges a fee to do that, and most banks don't want to pay. Thieves can use a child's identity over and over again. (If you just said, WTF?! then we both had the same reaction.)

There is some good news here. First and foremost, you can take action by safeguarding your Social Security number—never keep it in your wallet, and don't store it in your computer. You can also get monthly credit checks for both you and your children—even if they can't walk. I now do this myself, every month, whether I think

I need it or not. More good news: As a result of our report, the federal agents launched an investigation into Katie's case. Let's hope more will follow.

And the last bit of good news . . . When we first told folks about this issue, we offered free credit scans for the kids out there. Nearly 7,000 people took advantage of these free scans, and the results were eye-opening. One in ten—one in freaking ten!!!—found that someone else was using their child's Social Security number. This is not some oddball risk that could never happen to you. *One in ten*. Sign up for credit monitoring—yes, even for your newborn. You can sign up for credit checks for you *and* your kids (including newborns) with AllClear ID to monitor your credit and alert you to any problems. You can also use the three main credit agencies, Equifax, Experian, and TransUnion, which are required by federal law to provide you with one free copy of your credit report each year. (Note: If you request your own credit report, it has no effect on your score. When you *apply* for credit, the inquiry could impact your score.) One more thing—*always* keep your Social Security number private. And save that talk about teenage debt for when she wants to buy her first car . . . not when she's eating baby food.

Breaking into Hot Cars

A news alert just flashed across my screen. As I'm sitting here writing this entry, twin girls—only fifteen months old—just died in Georgia. They were left inside a car. The car heated up. The twins died.

The same thing might happen tomorrow. And the next day.

In many of these tragedies, the parent thinks that they'll only be gone from the car for "just a minute or two"—maybe to quickly duck inside a store—and then returns in horror. It happens by accident. You might think, *Okay, well, I don't live in the desert of New Mexico, so I have nothing to worry about.*

False. One child died in a car in Virginia, when the outdoor temperature was a pleasant 71 degrees. Another child died inside in a hot car in Georgia, in January, when the temperature was a brisk 52. Here's the terrifying thing: Even if it's comfy outside, the interior of a car can quickly reach temperatures as high as 100 degrees. Your car becomes a furnace.

To get a better handle on exactly how hot it can get—and to demonstrate the risks so that more parents will take this threat more seriously—I worked with an expert, Battalion Chief Abel Fernandez of the Miami-Dade Fire Rescue, to trap myself in a baking car.

The outside temperature is warm but not hot. Inside, I strap a bunch of wires to myself so Chief Fernandez can monitor my body temperature. I sit in the backseat and they close the doors. Then I whip out my phone and start a timer. Within thirty seconds I'm sweating. Within two minutes I'm fantasizing about a glass of ice water and trying to concentrate.

The temperature inside the car is now 100 degrees . . . and it has only been three minutes. Imagine if a baby was in here?

"Kids get hotter faster than adults do," says Chief Fernandez.

"So as hot as I am right now, a child would even be in more danger?" I ask, wiping sweat from my face.

He tells me the risk is at least twice as high.

I try to relax and adapt to the heat. Four minutes. Five minutes. My armpits break the seal and my shirt begins to soak with sweat. Chief Fernandez checks my vitals, ready to intervene when it gets too risky. After ten minutes, Fernandez looks at his monitor and says, "A hundred and one degrees. Now you're in a danger zone."

I nod, but I need to go a little longer. These little kids are put through hell, so I can last a few more minutes. From the backseat I look outside the car and see . . . *normalcy*. Outside it's just a normal day at a normal temperature, yet somehow I'm in an inferno. I touch the seat-belt buckle, and the metal is scalding hot. Whoa.

I realize that a young child would not be able to unbuckle the burning metal. Think about that. If a toddler is burning up, they would not be able to free themselves. It's wrenching.

"Your temperature is getting almost to 104," says Fernandez, growing more concerned. "It's too dangerous for you."

He calls it off. They open the door and I feel a blast of cool air. I gasp for breath and practically stumble outside the car.

My hair is plastered to my scalp, dripping buckets of sweat. My shirt is like a wet towel. I'm dizzy and disoriented. A child would be *twice* this hot and, if left alone, the child would be dead.

Let's say you pass a car and you see a child stuck inside. What do you do? After this experiment, my first instinct would be to literally punch in a car's window and free them.

Yet that wouldn't work.

The fire rescue department guides me to a car they've set up for this purpose, and asks me to "punch" the window in. "Go ahead, give it a try," says Lieutenant Marc Harrison.

I brace myself for the sound of shattered glass, grit my teeth, prepare for the inevitable bleeding, and strike the window with my elbow, hard, using all my force.

Thud.

Nothing. I feel powerless, and I imagine a kid burning up inside as I try and shatter the glass.

"You're not going to break it," says Lieutenant Harrison. "It's going to hurt you. It's probably going to break your elbow. And we don't want to break this window anyway, because if we do, glass shards are going to go all over the child. We want to use the other side."

KEY TAKEAWAY: If the child is sitting on the left, break the window on the right side of the car. *Don't* try to use your elbow or your fist. Instead, grab something from your trunk, like a tire iron or lug wrench. Where do you strike the window itself? You should strike the window in the bottom corner of the glass—that's the weakest part. *Not* in the center, which is what I would have guessed.

The fireman grabs the tire iron, sticks the pointy end at the bottom corner of the glass window, gives it a medium-strength tap, and I'm amazed to see the glass easily shatter. (Bonus tip: If you want to be extra prepared, you can pick up a "window breaker" from any big-box store for around $10 to $15, and keep it in your car just for this purpose. Use it for good, not evil.)

The whole experience throws me for a loop. As a parent I have strong feelings about this, and it's easy to vilify the moms and dads who are so careless that they, quite literally, leave their babies and children to die. But what I often see in these cases is that the parents are a lot like you and me, juggling their jobs, grocery shopping, mortgage payments, and trips to soccer practice.

Many hidden dangers in life are just that, hidden, and it's my hope that by exposing these risks, maybe the next time a dad in Georgia leaves his car on a pleasant afternoon, he takes his fifteen-month-old twins with him.

My School Security Test Should Scare the Hell Out of You

This book has been full of life-and-death topics that are important to me, but this one is on an entirely different level. My kids are in school. When I see a tragedy like the Sandy Hook school shooting, I'm no longer Jeff Rossen the Journalist, I'm Jeff Rossen the Dad. This stuff is horrifying. I honestly don't have the words to describe how much it sickens me. I know you feel the same.

As parents, we spend so much of our lives trying to protect our kids. We hold their hands when they cross the street, we buckle their seat belts, we double-lock the doors of our home. Yet Monday through Friday, for most of the day, they're out of our control.

So in the wake of Newtown, like millions of parents, I wondered, how safe *are* the schools? Have we learned any lessons? Are they taking the right precautions?

To test security protocols at schools, we set loose an intruder inside: me. How easy would it be for me to gain access to the classrooms and the kids themselves?

We start in a New Jersey suburb, where I stroll up to the front door of an elementary school and ring the buzzer. I come alone—no camera crew, no producers, just a random stranger.

"Hi, my name is Jeff," I say into the buzzer, "I just want to make an appointment with the principal?"

"Jeff who?"

"Jeff Rossen."

They buzz me inside the main doors—a troubling start—but before I can get to the classrooms, there's another set of locked doors. A staffer needs to physically escort me to the office. *Good.* These guys are taking safety seriously.

I head to a second school. At this one, security is even tighter, and a guard intercepts me the second I step on the premises, demanding that I show him my ID.

"You're gonna need it," he says, rightly suspicious.

"I'm going to need it?"

"Yes."

Good stuff. In fact, at four out of the five schools we tested, they kept me far away from the classrooms and the kids.

But then there's that one out of five.

I stroll up to the front door and ring the buzzer.

"Hi. Good morning," I say. "Here to see . . . go to the office?" I mutter, intentionally being vague just to see what would happen.

"Please come in."

"Thanks," I say, my heart sinking. *They didn't even ask my name.*

I walk through the front doors. There's no one here to escort me. The school's policy is for guests to find the office themselves, so I turn down a hallway and, within seconds, I see classrooms on every side of me. I roam the hallways. I walk by another classroom, another, and then the school gym. I hear the teachers giving lessons.

I hear the children laughing. I even peer inside a classroom. For a full two minutes I stroll down the hallways. No one stops me. No one questions me. No one even really *looks* at me. Only when I get to the office does a staffer flag me down.

Later, we show the footage to the school and the PTA, who calls our results "a wakeup call." We also show the footage to security expert Sal Lifrieri.

"This is incredibly problematic," says Lifrieri. "Something like this, two minutes of not being challenged, there's just too much harm you could have caused if you really had intent."

It'd be tempting to dismiss this school as a lone outlier, but others have found similar disturbing results. One reporter performed the same infiltration experiment in New York City. The undercover "intruder" was able to breeze past security and even join a gym full of kids. As he put it, "I have a harder time getting into my friend's apartment building."

Look, I get it. These schools are doing the best they can but, frankly, they have to do better. We all do. As a parent, I won't tolerate anything else—no parent should.

Okay, so that's the bad news.

Are there any schools doing it *right*? Is there any good news?

The Safest School in America

It turns out there is some good news. At the other end of the spectrum, we traveled to a school in Indiana—Southwestern High School—that some consider the "safest school in America." And they're not messing around.

"It used to be that education was the number-one thing that

schools did; now we need to keep our students safe first," said Dr. Paula Maurer, the superintendent at the time.

Their safety protocol is sometimes subtle, sometimes loud, and always top of mind. Take the hallways themselves. Tiny cameras are mounted on the ceilings, and not just one or two, here and there, but *everywhere*. They can monitor everything. And guess who's watching the footage from those cameras? Cops. Real time. The cameras are remotely connected to the sheriff's department (just ten miles away), allowing the authorities to track an intruder in real time.

Each teacher has their own panic button. "We all wear a fob in case there's a security breach," explains one teacher, showing me an electronic button that she wears on a lanyard around her neck. "We can push this button, and the entire alarm system goes off in the school."

There's more. Each classroom is wired with a box that's also hooked up to the sheriff's department. The teacher can flip it to *Help* if they actually see the suspect, or they can flip it to *Safe* if the kids are out of danger.

They've also trained the students. "What would you do if there was an active shooter here right now?" I ask the teacher.

"Security breach!" she yells.

Instantly the kids react. They scramble from their desks and all converge in one corner of the classroom, they duck and cover, and they even flip some of their desks to the side to be used as shields. The whole operation takes maybe five seconds. It's breathtaking. These kids would give the marines a run for their money.

I look closer, and see that all the kids are now behind a line of red tape on the ground. Interesting. What does the red line mean?

"The red line is a security measure, and that's in place because if we stand behind this red line, if there's a shooter at the door, they cannot see the children."

Brilliant. I look from the door to the red line to the kids who are ducking and covering—she's right. They've measured the line of sight from the doorway, and they've figured out precisely where to assemble the kids so they'd be in a shooter's blind spot. Clever. Some security measures are expensive, and some are as cheap as a roll of tape.

"And this is something schools can do right now, this red line on the ground?"

"Absolutely."

Okay, it's time to put this school to the same test as before—again I would play the intruder. How far could I get? Could I get into a classroom?

For one thing, it's unlikely I could even get past the front doors (which, by the way, are bullet-resistant.) But let's say I somehow did. Again I roam the hallways, but this time I'm being tracked by the cameras, and the police can follow my every move.

As I walk down the hallway I think about going into a class-room . . . but I can't. The school instantly goes on lockdown, turning each classroom into a tiny fortress. Every last classroom is locked, triggered by the intruder alarm.

I take another step forward and then . . . *Boom!* A blast of smoke fires from the ceiling. *Boom!* Then another. *Boom!* Smoke instantly fills the hallway. I feel like I'm under attack. I'm blinded. A loud siren blares. I'm completely disoriented—literally deaf and blind.

All I can see is a cloudy haze of white smoke, as I have just triggered the school's secret weapon, its "hot zone" that can be remotely activated by the police. The beauty of it is that the authorities can track wherever the intruder goes, and they can keep unleashing these hot zones to disorient him, redirect him, and push him to a place where they can intercept him. He can barely see his own hand, much less the students.

It's truly a game changer.

This security, of course, doesn't come cheap. The system costs $400,000, soup to nuts and, because it's a test school, the security company donated a big chunk of it. And the school received a government grant to pay for the rest. But as the superintendent told me, if schools can afford to pay for football fields and stadiums, they can find money for this. And as for the kids? I asked if the security drills scare them and they said, "No." They love it. It makes them feel safe, and they say the drills are empowering.

The Claw Machine
Hates My Son

George Washington. Apple pie. Fireworks. And on this list of things that are quintessentially *American*, we must add The Claw. They're at every arcade, bowling alley, amusement park, and diner in the country.

But are they rigged? Judging by my own rotten luck with The Claw, it sure seems like it. And since this is clearly a topic of life and death, I decided to unleash the full investigative powers of the *Today* show to get to the bottom of it. I consulted with a Claw Expert (yes, that actually exists), hunted down Claw owner's manuals to inspect the fine print, and even purchased my own Claw machine to set up at home. (My kids: thrilled. My wife: less so.)

Okay, first off, just in case you are one of the seven people in America who has not played The Claw, this is how it works: You plunk a quarter (or more) into a machine, then you use a joystick to control the claw, and you maneuver this claw to try and pick up stuffed animals, toys, or sometimes high-value items like iPhones and jewelry. It looks so easy. Yet it always feels that *just* when you are about to snatch that purple rhinoceros, somehow it slips through your metal fingers.

"Absolutely not fair," says Claw expert Jeremy Hambly, who, amazingly, has analyzed hundreds of Claw machines. He runs the website and YouTube channel ClawStruck, which breaks down the inner workings of the machines in glorious detail. "Crane operators can change the strength of the claw throughout the day. They can even set them to pay out at different rates . . . One in fifty means you will not win unless they say so."

To demonstrate this, we hatch a highly scientific experiment: In my apartment, I put some money in my shiny new Claw machine and try to pick up an orange stuffed animal. I use the joystick to bring the claw under the animal's legs, pick it up, and . . . it falls right back into the pile. Same thing happens the second time. Third. Fourth. Fortieth. I let my son Blake try . . . no luck. He frowns in disappointment. Like father, like son—we're both powerless to beat The Claw.

Then Hambly shows me The Claw's dirty little secret. He opens a control panel and shows me two knobs. "If the operator wants to change how the machine reacts, there's two knobs inside here," he says, pointing at the controls. "One is for the *strength* of The Claw when it picks [the toy] up, and the other is for how strong it carries it to the chute." These controls, effectively, let the owner calibrate the payout. The very same machine can be a loose winner or a stingy trap.

Hambly adjusts the knobs. "Max claw strength," he says with satisfaction.

"Max claw strength?" I ask.

He nods. Okay, max claw strength. *Let's do this.* Once again, I aim for my old nemesis, the orange stuffed animal. Once again I use the joystick, pick it up . . . and this time I easily drag it to the chute. Winner! I try again—and I win again. Suddenly I'm a Claw Master, ready to compete in the Claw Olympics.

Hambly explains that other models are far more sophisticated, calculating exactly *when* it's time for someone to win, which gives frustrated players *just* enough motivation to keep throwing quarters away. One of the Claw owner's manuals even bluntly states to arcade owners that "Managing profit is made easy." That sounds awesome . . . until you realize that their gain is your loss.

"There needs to be more oversight," says Hambly. "Right now there's basically none, and if a machine is only going to pay out one in every fifty times, they should have to post [the odds] right on it for people."

Yet there's one person who isn't that concerned with the issue of oversight: my son, Blake. Now that the setting is on maximum claw strength, he plays again and he wins right away. A huge smile lights up his face. He wins again, smiles even wider, and he keeps winning and keeps smiling. He's old enough to *know* that The Claw can be rigged, but that's irrelevant when the rhinoceros tumbles to the chute. Those quarters purchased a shot of pure, unfiltered joy and, as he proudly clutches all of his new stuffed animals, for one moment I feel like I'm five years old again, too.

6

VACATION UNDERCOVER

A**H, THE BEACH! VACATION! WATER SPORTS!** Time to relax and take it easy. Except that maybe you'll get stranded at sea, or the jewelry you purchase might be fake, or the maid isn't really changing your sheets. (I'm always an optimist.) So before you pack your swimsuit, read on. . . .

- ◎ Are "All-Inclusives" Really the Best Deal?
- ◎ Stranded in the Ocean
- ◎ Sky-High SPF: Is It Really Worth It?
- ◎ Drowning Myths and Tips Revealed
- ◎ Rip-Off Alert: Your Jewelry May Be Fake
- ◎ Is the Hotel Maid Really Changing Your Sheets?
- ◎ The Great American Germ Cruise

Are "All-Inclusives" Really the Best Deal?

When Danielle and I are trying to plan a vacation, we're often torn between two options: 1) The "all-inclusive" plan from a hotel; and 2) Pay-as-you-go. (Of course, usually we go with Secret Option 3: The vacation was just a pipe dream, reality hits us, and we stay home instead.)

The all-inclusives sure *seem* like a good deal. All the food you can eat! Unlimited snorkeling! Never-ending frozen daiquiris—enough to make your brain freeze! I've always wondered which option was truly the better deal, but I had no real way of finding out. Who would? The resorts have concluded that no tourist is willing, able, or curious enough to blow tons of money and *conduct an actual experiment* to figure out which option is the better deal.

Heh-heh.

Thanks to my corporate card and some very understanding bosses, my producer Lindsey and I book two identical vacations. Our mission? A three-day trip to the Dominican Republic, staying at a gorgeous luxury resort. I'm a giver like that.

Posing as an ordinary tourist, Lindsey books a room using an all-inclusive rate. I book an identical room the regular way, using pay-as-you-go. We coordinate the vacation to make sure that we order precisely the same things. The same food, the same drinks, the same activities. This involves a fair amount of negotiation, as she wins the battle of wine selection, and I veto the watermelon martini.

At dinner, I ask our waiter, "Can I have the stuffed chicken breast?"

"I will also have the stuffed chicken breast," Lindsey says.

"I'll have a Sauvignon blanc," I say.

"I'll have the same thing!" Lindsey says with a smile.

At breakfast, the buffet overflows with fruits, french toast, and made-on-demand omelets. Delicious.

"Really good," Lindsey agrees.

Then the bill arrives. I shake my head when I see it—$37. Those hash browns were tasty, but . . . they really get you for breakfast.

Lindsey gets up from the table, not a care in the world. "Mine's included, enjoy paying your bill!" She's sassy like that.

After brunch it's time for an important meeting—reading magazines by the pool. Now, I wouldn't do this on a normal Tuesday, but we *are* posing as tourists and we *are* trying to simulate a real vacation, so, for the integrity of our experiment, we both order margaritas.

Twelve dollars for me, plus tax and tip.

Zero dollars for Lindsey. She sips hers, and it looks like it somehow even *tastes* better when it feels free.

We go kayaking and we go snorkeling. (Thirty-four dollars for me, zero dollars for Lindsey.) We take full advantage of the swim-up bar, ordering more drinks. Later we splurge at dinner, enjoying a candlelit Italian meal, ordering plenty of apps and wine and dessert. Some musicians serenade the two of us, strumming their guitars, hoping for a mood of romance. We laugh awkwardly and I smile politely at the singer, figuring that I can't really say, "We're not a couple, but we're here on an experiment to evaluate the resort's pricing structure."

And then, on Day 3, the main event: We check out and receive our bills. We're both in complete suspense.

Lindsey's bill: $1,996.80.

I stare at the envelope that contains my bill. Would it be higher or lower? As I slowly open the envelope, I felt like a poor man's Oscar presenter.

My bill: $1,621.20.

"Boom! I got the better deal!" I say to Lindsey, always gracious in victory. "I win!"

To recap: For the past three days I had made no effort to be frugal. We were *stuffed* the entire time, and we each had—ah—five drinks a day. This was an indulgent vacation . . . and it was *still* cheaper than the all-inclusive. I saved $375, and if I had been booking a trip with my wife, I would have saved $750 for the two of us. (Cue deep-voice, fast-talking announcer guy: "Prices may vary. Do your own research.")

Lindsey looks at her check, frowns, and reality sinks in. "Obviously, I'm still expensing this."

Stranded in the Ocean

Sometimes my "vacation research" involves all-inclusive resorts, and sometimes it involves, well, the absolute worst-case vacation scenario. Imagine that you're on vacation and on a boat. Then imagine that you're somehow stranded at sea. How do you survive?

This is more common than you might think. Every year, the brave men and women of the U. S. Coast Guard rescue *thousands* of people stranded at sea. How dangerous are the rescue attempts? What does it feel like to get yanked from the water? And if you're somehow stuck at sea, what can you do to boost your odds of survival?

I decide to personally find out. For better or worse, I might be the first person in the history of planet Earth to *voluntarily* get stranded at sea, and then rescued by the Coast Guard.

The night before they toss me in the ocean, the Coast Guard gives me some basic water-survival tests. They have me swim four laps in a pool. No problem. They ask me to tread water for ten minutes. Easy peasy. How hard could this be?

Then, off the shore of Miami, they drop me in the open ocean and leave me to sink or swim.

For maybe .000000000001 seconds I remain calm and start treading water. So far, so good. And then, because I'm a seasoned reporter and a self-proclaimed tough guy, I think, *I'm going to die.*

First off, treading water in the ocean is twice as hard as doing it in a pool. The waves seem to pull your body every which way, you are blinded, water gushes into your nostrils, and the panic sets in. The panic is not just psychological; it physically affects you, making you feel like you're swimming upstream. But, of course, you *are* swimming upstream, because gravity is trying to pull you down to your watery death.

I look to the sky—where's that damn Coast Guard chopper? Did they forget about me? More water shoots into my nose. My eyes are stinging. I accidentally swallow a gulp.

We underestimate the power of water. Fire gets all the glory, but when it comes to the risk of getting killed, water can be just as terrifying. And I don't say this as someone who's afraid of swimming; I grew up on Long Island, surrounded by beaches, and I loved to jump in the waves and go swimming with my dad.

As I wait for the Coast Guard chopper (What if they never come? What if they can't see me, as I'm just a tiny dot in the distance?) I realize something else about water: *You don't have any options.* So often in life we might have a problem and we think we don't have any options, but usually we do. Maybe your boss is being a jerk or your spouse is being unkind and you think *I don't have any good options*, but really, you do. You will go on living. But when your lungs fill with water and you get yanked into the maw of the ocean? You have no options.

Well, *almost* no options. There's one trick that's useful. Even though I'm panicking, I remember that the best way to conserve energy is something called the "dead man's float." (To be honest, I'm not sure the phrase "dead man" is the best choice for boosting your confidence, but whatever.)

This is how you do the "dead man's float": Lie facedown in the water and keep your face underwater. Every so often, you pop up for air. It's an efficient way to get air to your lungs, and you don't have to waste energy by kicking your arms and legs.

I finally see the helicopter whooshing through the sky toward me—I say "finally," but it was probably only three minutes—and I feel a jolt of elation. A Coast Guard diver, wearing a wet suit and flippers, dives out of the chopper and swims toward me. They drop a safety cable, launch a smoke signal, and a puff of orange smoke fills the sky—I would think it looked really cool and cinematic if I didn't worry that I might die.

By now, when we see these videos on the news, we think, "Crisis over. They're safe." Not true. And I'm about to see why.

It's almost impossible to hear anything. Helicopters are *loud*.

The waves crash into me and blind me, whack me, disorient me. Thanks to the tsunami-like winds caused by the whirling blades of the helicopter, *even the Coast Guard rescuer* has a tough time spotting the safety cable. I'm swallowing salt water like it's my job. Then, when he finds the cable, he has to dive underwater to fasten me, and when I can't see him, once again I feel a sliver of panic—*Is he gone?*

Finally he hooks me to the cable and I feel a pang of relief as he signals to the chopper to pull us up. Soon my head emerges from the water, then my arms, chest, legs, and now I'm hanging by a cable above the water, swaying back and forth, getting higher, higher, and higher—a hundred times scarier than the world's longest bungee jump. Rational thoughts are not part of this equation. *What if the cable isn't tied correctly?! What if my weight pulls the chopper down? What if the rescuer needs to get rescued?* And did I mention I'm scared of heights?

Finally, they pull us safely into the chopper. I slap the Coast Guard rescuer a weary high five and pull him in for a bear hug. Even though I was operating in a somewhat controlled environment, the whole thing filled me with deadly anxiety, and when I am safe in the chopper I feel true joy. The rescuer might as well be wearing a cape and tights—he truly looks like a superhero. And these guys *are* heroes. To our overseas troops we say "Thank you for your service." The Coast Guard deserves that same recognition.

This is yet another example of why I hate the advice "don't panic." Even though I knew the Coast Guard was just minutes away, and even though, logically, I knew that I would almost certainly live, I still felt the liquid fear. And if I ever get stranded and rescued again, I know that I will *again* panic, but I also know that I have what it takes to survive—you do, too. And, to my wife, I say this: Don't worry, I will never again volunteer for this. (Probably.)

Sky-High SPF: Is It Really Worth It?

I'm going to tell you something I've never shared before. I had skin cancer.

One day I noticed a tiny brown mark above my belly button. "You should get it checked out," Danielle told me. Problem is, I'm stubborn.

"Oh give me a break," I told her, "It's fine. I don't have time to see the dermatologist. It doesn't look that bad."

"If you were on TV right now, you'd be telling someone to get this checked," she snapped back, "so why won't you take care of yourself?"

I promised to keep an eye on it. (Code for "Get off my back.") Months passed. I didn't see much of a change. We look at our bodies every day and don't notice those incremental changes. We're mired in our routines. Shower. Brush hair. Brush teeth. Deodorant. Get out the door. We never really *look* at ourselves. But one day, about two months after Danielle's first plea, I remember coming out of the shower, catching a glimpse of myself while toweling off, and I freaked out. The spot had become bigger. Much bigger. And darker. Much darker. So I finally gave in. I got tests, and soon the doctor told me it was melanoma. The worst possible kind of skin cancer you can get. As an added bonus, this increases your chances of getting cancer again in the future.

The doctors dug it out, they did more biopsies, they dug deeper, they did more biopsies, they dug even deeper, and they kept digging until they got a clean reading. Now, every six months I'm in the doctor's office for a scan, ever vigilant, waiting for it to come back.

Sunscreen is a big part of my life—it's as essential as a toothbrush. Yet, when I go to the store and look at the sunscreen, I'm confused. There are a billion options. SPF 30, 50, 70, 80, even 110. There are creams and sprays, tubes and cans. There are practically more versions of sunscreen than there are brands of breakfast cereal. (Aside: Does the planet really need thirty-seven different types of berry cereal? Look for that in the sequel.)

The higher the SPF, it seems, the higher the price tag. Especially when kids are concerned, we're tempted to pay a premium to avoid burns and blisters and skin cancer. And the companies know it.

But is the extra SPF worth it? Even for those, like me, with cancer risks, does it make any difference?

"I tell my patients SPF over 50 is useless," says Dr. Ellen Marmur, a dermatologist at Mount Sinai. "Save your money and stick with the 30 to 50 plus." It turns out that *double the SPF* does not mean *double the protection*; if you buy SPF 100 instead of SPF 50, you're actually getting about *one percent* more protection. There's no evidence that anything over SPF 50 protects you any better . . . even though they cost an arm and a leg.

How can the sunscreen companies get away with this? I decide to go straight to the industry group representing the sunscreen companies, the Personal Care Products Council, and speak with Farah Ahmed, its spokeswoman at the time. "Have you seen evidence that anything over SPF 50 plus gives you better protection?" I ask her.

"Well, because we are not part of that dialogue," stammers Ahmed, "that's not an area that I have gotten into—"

"You're representing the industry?" I remind her.

"That's true."

"Have you seen any science that shows that anything over SPF 50 better protects you?"

A slight pause. "That scientific door I have not opened because there is a debate going on," she says. And that scientific door, it turns out, led the FDA to propose new rules that would ban the sky-high labels that confuse and mislead consumers.

How about the claims of "waterproof" or "sweatproof"?

The science says that your sunscreen is just about as "sweatproof" as it is "bulletproof." Dr. Marmur says that "waterproof and sweatproof are not true. If you go in the water and you swim, or in the ocean or pool, and you come out, you've lost that sunscreen."

This has changed the way I buy sunscreen, and again, I don't say this lightly. Given my melanoma, in the past I would always err on the side of caution and splurge on SPF 90 or SPF 110; if they sold SPF 5,000, I would probably spend good money on that, too. But it's just bogus marketing, plain and simple. These companies make money on the backs of our fears, and as a cancer survivor, frankly, this pisses me off.

Thanks in part to investigations like this, the FDA did ban the use of the terms "waterproof" and "sweatproof." Now companies are only allowed to use "water resistant" as long as they indicate how long it remains effective.

Score a tiny victory for the good guys. And my wife, who is always right.

Drowning Myths and Tips Revealed

Did you know more kids die in swimming pools than from guns each year? Yep, it's true. And, for kids between the ages of one and four, accidental drowning is the number one killer. Every year there are 3,536 deaths by drowning, or about ten *per day*. (Even scarier? Kids under five have the highest risk.) So if the unthinkable happens, do you know how to save your drowning child's life?

This is how.

Here's the first thing to know: Drowning is often *silent*. This makes it especially scary. I always thought that when a kid is drowning they would be splashing, flailing, and maybe screaming for help.

"Unfortunately, that's not the case," says Jeff Thompson, a certified lifeguard. "They really can't breathe, so they really can't be calling out for help." In reality, most of the action is happening *under* the water; the child will look like she's trying to climb stairs, with her arms going up and down.

WHEN SOMEONE IS DROWNING: Scream for somebody to call 911. Next, use something like a pool skimmer, or your arm to get them out. (Bonus tip: Always keep the pool skimmer handy, ideally on the deck somewhere.)

Then, pull the child up and out of the water. Gently roll her over on her back and check to see if she's conscious. And you know how, in the movies, everyone immediately starts doing mouth-to-mouth?

Don't do that.

"We *don't* want to do that," explains Thompson. "Focus just on chest compressions, because that's going to keep the brain alive until the ambulance gets here." Now, if you're like me, you probably aren't totally sure what "focus on chest compressions" means. So here's your game plan: You'll want to find the base of the rib cage, two fingers above that little notch at the bottom. Place the heel of one hand there (at the base of rib cage), and the other hand on top of it, lacing your fingers. And as Thompson explains it, "you compress the chest at about a hundred compressions a minute like you're trying to squeeze the water out of a wet Nerf ball."

"This looks like it could hurt somebody," I tell him, a little confused.

"It can break ribs. But it's going to keep them alive."

Fair enough. And it sounds like a cliché, but seconds really do matter, especially when someone is drowning. One key variable is often the difference between life and death: *How many seconds was the brain without oxygen?* So, when in doubt, take action.

Luckily, you do have another thing on your side: technology. Because, let's face it, when you have a swimming pool, there are two different realities of parental supervision:

1) The *ideal* reality, where you are keeping your kid in sight at all times, ever vigilant, ready to spring into action at a moment's notice; and

2) *Actual* reality, where, of course, you're doing your best to make sure they don't fall into the pool, but you're also juggling things like cooking, or cleaning, or going to the bathroom, or trying to wrangle the *other* kid, or maybe they're supposed to be upstairs but then they sneak outside, or maybe you simply turn away for ten seconds. I'm the first to admit that I'll check my iPhone or iPad while my kids are running around—who *doesn't* do this?

For better or worse, of course, we live in the actual reality. But I've found three gizmos that can help make your pool as safe as possible, trimming the risk and adding some peace of mind:

1) Pool WatchDog

Imagine if you paid some teenager ten bucks to just stare at your pool, always, without blinking, and to yell if something happens. That's the Pool WatchDog. It's a camera that literally is just trained right on your pool, and if something goes in the water, it zaps an alert to your smartphone. (Handy for pets, too.)

2) Poolguard Safety Buoy

This bad boy floats in the water, and it actually senses motion inside the pool. Any little ripple will set it off. Let's say you're in the kitchen and you *think* your kid is doing homework in her room, but it turns out she ran outside. If, God forbid, she falls into the pool, the water buoy would detect the motion and send a loud alarm through speakers you install in the house.

3) Safety Turtle

It's a wristband that your kid can wear. If I put it on Skyler, Sloane, or Blake, I'll know that the second their wrist hits the water, I'll be notified with a loud shrieking alarm. Let's say, for example, you're going to a large family barbecue and there's a pool, and you know your kids won't be in sight at all times. This gives you one extra level of safety.

All three of these cost less than $200 each. None of them can fully replace the importance of eyes-on-kid, but they're useful for those of us who live in the real world, not the fantasy world.

Rip-Off Alert: Your Jewelry May Be Fake

When I'm on vacation, my guard is down. I'm in a great mood. I'm relaxed, I'm going with the flow, and my most complicated decision is whether to order a frozen margarita or a frozen daiquiri. Especially when I'm on a romantic vacation with my wife, the whole goal is to reconnect, to soak in the sunshine, to laugh, and maybe, sure, to splurge a little. (Yep, even though I'm a consummate cheapskate, even *I* will open the wallet on vacations. Who doesn't?)

So if Danielle and I are strolling through a beach town, arm in arm (Okay, we haven't done that in years, but go with it), maybe we'll step into the large, glittering jewelry stores with the bright lights and the giant glass display cases. There are bargains! There are steals! Normally I wouldn't give these guys the time of day. But when I'm floating in paradise? Sure, why not live a little? I'll enter the shop, listen to the jeweler's sales pitch, and convince myself, *This would cost a LOT more money back home. I'm getting a bargain.*

But imagine that you get home, and find out that the jewelry you just bought was a scam? I'm not the only one who had that suspicion. Viewers e-mail me with the same question, feeling that they've been burned.

It's time to go undercover.

My producer Jovanna, always up for an adventure, volunteers to travel with me to Cozumel, Mexico, where she pretends to be a tourist who wants to buy some sapphires. (This is not much of an acting challenge—Jovanna likes her jewelry.) We head to the main shopping district, the kind of bazaar that sells T-shirts and souvenirs and other knickknacks.

Jovanna's eyes are drawn to some blue sapphire rings. Even I can tell they're pretty. The shopkeeper tells us the ring would cost $750 in the United States . . . but they would sell it to us for $350.

Score! I love me a good bargain.

But here's what the shopkeepers don't know: Jovanna is joined by a hidden shopper, Karen DeHass, a certified gemologist with more than forty years of experience. She later inspects these sapphires with a tiny microscope, putting them through a battery of tests.

"This isn't even a sapphire," says Karen. "It's blue-colored glass."

"What is this worth?" I ask.

"The whole thing is worth about twenty-five dollars," Karen says. "It's garbage. I wouldn't put it in my fish tank."

Ouch. Not even the fish tank.

Next stop: Florida. We rack up some frequent-flyer miles and head to Key West, again sending Jovanna and Karen into the jewelry store. Jovanna buys a pair of diamond-studded earrings—she's had worse days at the office—that the shopkeeper says would normally cost $4,400 . . . but gives her a deal for $3,200.

Then Karen, our gemologist, gives them a full inspection. "They're not even the color or clarity that they said they were. They're much worse." Karen says we overpaid by $800. Same thing at another store, where, according to Karen, they're worth "less than *half*" of what we paid.

THE TAKEAWAY HERE: Even when you're in vacation mode, it makes sense to be a savvy shopper . . . especially when you're plunking down serious cash.

Beware your "vacation goggles," which can temporarily impair your judgment. (Bonus problem: When you return to the United States, you have to pay *taxes* on those overpriced stones, adding insult to injury.)

Okay, but what about when you're shopping for jewelry at home and *not* wearing vacation goggles? You would think that you're protected. You would think that reputable stores are, well, reputable.

Usually that's the case. But *rubies*, it turns out, are an altogether different beast.

Again, we go on a shopping spree, this time for red rubies back home in America. First we hit up a major department store, where the salesperson shows us a gorgeous ruby that emits a deep red. He says that the ruby has "lead glass," but then assures us that it's "a real ruby."

Later, we have this "real ruby" analyzed by two world-renowned gemologists, Antoinette Matlins and Gary Smith. They squint into microscopes and analyze the jewelry.

"These are *not* rubies," announces Matlins. "Period."

Whoa. This wasn't from some random shopkeeper in Cozumel; this was from a large American retailer.

At another giant chain, the saleswoman never even mentions the lead glass, instead telling us, "It is real. It is natural." The price tag is $1,200. And once again, it is *not* a natural ruby. It's filled with glass.

With the naked eye it's very, very difficult to tell the difference. If I show you a spread of five real rubies and one that's filled with glass, I bet you couldn't tell the difference. (I couldn't.) One telltale sign, though, is that up close, the glass rubies have air bubbles trapped inside. And, as gemologist Gary Smith tells me, "there's never an air bubble in a natural ruby."

Here's an even better test. Gary Smith takes a real 100-percent natural ruby and dunks it in a cleaning solution—the kind you would find at any jewelers. Just minutes later it still looks the same—red, clear, beautiful.

Then he does the same thing to the "natural ruby" that the retailer sold us, the one that's actually filled with glass. Minutes later he takes it out, and even I, a jewelry rookie, can tell that it's garbage. It's cracked, ugly, and literally falling apart.

There is a bit of good news here. As a result of our investigation, two retailers told NBC News that they're retraining their sales associates. Two others offered refunds for dissatisfied customers. And one went even further, removing any reference to the word "genuine" in their advertising. I love making a difference for you.

But what should you do if a salesperson says to you, "This is a *natural ruby*" or "It's genuine" or "It's real"?

FIRST: Get it in writing.

As gemologist Gary Smith advises, make sure that your receipt has the words "genuine" or "natural" or "untreated."

SECOND: Most jewelry counters will actually have a magnifying glass. Those aren't just for show. You can use it to inspect the stone—the salesperson should let you—and if you see any little round air bubbles, that means it could be glass-filled or reconstructed.

"Mother nature doesn't put 'air bubbles' in anything," explains Smith. "Consumers can spot them."

Is the Hotel Maid Really Changing Your Sheets?

Think about when you first walk into a hotel room. It looks clean, tidy, crisp. The bed is made, the sink is spotless, and the towels are folded in a nice white stack. Part of me has always wondered, is it *really* clean? Like many people, I try to avoid the bed's top blanket, as lord knows what's on that thing.

What about the pillows? I mean, that's about as personal as it gets. Your face is smushed against the pillowcase, and it rubs against your lips, your cheeks, your nostrils. People drool on pillows. And, oh God, what about the bathroom? How many thousands of people have used that very sink and that very toilet? The glass cups have those nice paper covers that look so sanitary, so sterile, and they practically taunt, "Drink from me, I'm clean!" But *are they?* Call it journalistic curiosity or call it a neurosis—I'm skeptical.

I launch another experiment. My team sets up hidden cameras in a variety of hotels, from the cheapest motels to the suites of four-star luxury. Then we make it look like I slept in each room, which, I have to admit, is a good deal of fun. I toss some towels on the floor, I rumple the bed, and I pour drinks in the glasses and take a few sips—finally, a work-related excuse to raid the minibar! (Alas, it was only soda.) When finished, I look around the dirty room in satisfaction. Good job, Rossen. Nailed it.

At one hotel, I pick up the phone and call downstairs. "Hi, can you send housekeeping up to clean my room?"

I step out of the room . . . but here's what the hidden cameras show. The maid quickly strips the bed of the dirty sheets, tossing the pillows to the side. Then she replaces the sheets with new ones. Okay, so far so good. Then she takes the *old* pillows and puts them back on the bed, giving each one a quick fluff, not even changing the pillowcases. Wait. Did I see that right? I rewind the video and watch it again—yep. She just put my old dirty pillows back on the bed. *Whoa.* These are the pillows that we drool on. I stay in a lot of hotels. If they're not cleaning the pillowcases, you could be exposed to my drool (not that I drool).

Now she heads to the bathroom. She scrubs everything with hot water and disinfectant—I start to relax—and she dries the toilet with a towel. But then she uses the *same* towel to dry the shower and then the *same* dirty, toilet-tainted towel to wipe the counter near the sink. Let me repeat that: *She used the same towel to scrub the toilet and the counter*—the surface where you put your toothbrush.

But maybe they run a tighter ship elsewhere? We switch hotels, and in that room, the maid changes the sheets and then, just like before, she plops the old, used pillow back onto the bed. Two maids, two dirty pillows.

Am I being unreasonable here? For a second opinion I reach out to hospitality expert Jacob Tomsky, who spent a decade working in hotels. He tells us that housekeepers should, of course, change the pillowcases. "That's what you sleep on. And what really bothered me was that she put the pillowcase on a dirty chair. . . . That just gets it even more dirty."

Next, I watch some footage from my dirty room at a third, more upscale hotel. The maid collects all of my dirty glasses, puts them in the sink, and lets them soak in hot water. Then she grabs the dirty towels off the floor, and *uses one of the dirty towels* to dry the glasses.

Let me repeat: She used the gross, dirty towel to dry the drinking glasses!

She then puts the paper lids on top to show that they've been "sanitized." As the cherry on top, she uses the same dirty towel to wipe the counter, toilet, and tub. She never uses any soap. But who needs soap when you have air freshener? Before leaving, she spritzes the room so that it smells nice and fresh.

After this horror show, the company that owns two of the hotels told us that health, safety, and comfort are top priorities. It performs regular inspections and is working to review standards. Another hotel told us cleanliness is a focal point of its operations, and it has procedures and guidelines in place to make sure things are sanitized properly. That hotel plans to conduct a review and address any infractions. We'll see.

To clarify, I feel for the maids. They have so many rooms to clean and they're on their feet all day, scrubbing, mopping, folding, and most of them do an excellent job, and we should thank them and tip them. But some take shortcuts.

"Is [it the maids'] fault that they're missing things?" I ask Tomsky, the hospitality expert. "Or is it management's fault for not checking?"

"Management should stay vigilant and check and make sure that they have everything they need to do the job," says Tomsky. "Honestly, that's why spot checks are good. And even these hidden-camera things are good."

Sigh. I guess that's a silver lining—I'm hopeful that hotels can change their behavior. But I'm not counting on it.

Travel experts advise that when you call housekeeping you should be specific. Tell them, "Hey, can you please change *all* the bedding, including the pillowcases?" Or "We used the glasses, can you bring fresh cups?"

I no longer drink from the cups unless they're the plastic ones, which guarantees I'm the first one to take a sip. As for the Pillow Problem? Trickier. I thought about traveling with my own personal pillow, but if I do that, suddenly I've turned into a guy who walks around with his own pillow, and then I have even bigger problems. I guess I'll opt for the drool.

The Great American
Germ Cruise

In the name of research, I bravely volunteered to spend four days on a luxury Caribbean cruise ship, the kind that's packed with food and drinks and sun-soaked paradise. I'm a martyr like that. And I brought along the entire Rossen Reports team for two important reasons: 1) Going undercover, we had a secret mission to test the boat for germs; and 2) Now I don't have to buy them Christmas presents.

Germs are a real threat, especially when you have thousands of people all jammed together on a floating petri dish. Just ask Tina Krasner, who was on a boat when norovirus swept her cruise ship. "That sickness spread like wildfire, so fast," Tina tells us, still looking shaken. "It was worse than *The Exorcist*, to be honest with you."

On that cheery note, time to cruise! We arm ourselves with the usual vacation gear of swimsuits, sunscreen, and official "bacteria meters." These are handheld electronic gizmos that instantly analyze the results of cotton swabs. You just wipe a Q-tip-looking thingy on a surface, stick the Q-tip in the bacteria meter, and it spits out an electronic reading. Experts say that anything over one hundred is unacceptable.

We first head to the same place everyone heads to on a cruise: the food. I look at the frozen-yogurt machine and watch everyone touch the same handle. That must be filthy, right? My producer Josh, posing as a normal passenger who wants a frozen treat, tries to act nonchalant, casual, as he discreetly swabs the handle with his Q-tip. (Never mind the fact that this "normal passenger" just happens to be wearing latex gloves. Not weird at all.) He then dips the swab into the bacteria meter, and to our surprise . . . it's clean! Good start.

Then we have dinner at the restaurant and covertly swab the menu, fully embracing my new role as James Bond. *(Rossen. Jeff Rossen.)* The food menu is clean, too. But just to be scientifically responsible, I order more food and more drinks for the table, and then some dessert. Diligence is important.

So far, so good. But could the entire ship *really* be that sanitary? We dug deeper. As a golden sunset enchants the ship's passengers, we skulk around with our latex gloves and our Q-tips and our bacteria detectors—the life of the party. We head to the casino. I've never had much luck with slot machines, so I'm not that surprised when we swab the handle, stick it in the gizmo, and the reading comes back as. . . . 373, or over *three times* the acceptable limit of 100. (Yet one more reason not to gamble all your money away. . . .)

Same problem on the ship's elevators. The elevator buttons score a 370, teeming with bacteria. "Cruises are like an island in the sea," says Dr. Robert Glatter. "Essentially everyone is living together, working together, eating together, putting them at risk for passing infections to one another."

Hmmm. Maybe we'd have better luck by the pool? Instead of working on her tan, my producer, Jovanna, stealthily swabs a lounge chair, and it comes back with a whopping 773. That's more than *seven times* the acceptable limit.

It gets worse. We head to the holy grail of cruise freebies, the buffet, and swab the serving handles that everyone is using to scoop their all-you-can-eat eggs and bacon. I look at the greasy eggs, the dirty handle, and then look back at the restaurant and see everyone eating with their hands. *I don't even want to know* what kind of germs are on that handle.

But, of course, I want to know. We swab it and test it. Remember how experts say the acceptable limit is 100? The buffet handle comes back at *2,102.* The score is so high that it almost can't be shown on the bacteria meter, which has a display that usually shows just two or three digits. It was so high that we sent it to a certified lab and they found total coliform. Just how bad is total coliform?

"It's very bad," says Dr. Glatter. "These are bacteria that live in our gut, in our GI tract. They make you really sick."

It's poop.

"What can these cruise lines do?" I ask him.

"What they can do first is have someone serve you at the salad bar or the buffet."

Ah-ha! So *that's* why I always insist on people serving me. (Kidding. Sort of.) Okay, all of that said, there is some good news here. About 22 million people cruise each year, and the number of people who get sick, usually, is in the low thousands. And when we reached out to the cruise industry, they told us that they go through stringent and scientifically valid inspections by federal health officials. They said the industry has an exemplary record and they continue to raise the bar on health and sanitation practices.

But still. On my next cruise I'm bringing extra wipes, hand sanitizer, and I'm washing my hands even more than usual. After all, it's "worse than *The Exorcist.*" Yet the real tragedy here? The germs were so high that, in the end, I felt bad and I still bought the team Christmas presents. And I'm Jewish!

7

EVERYDAY LIFE
HACKS

PROBLEMS POP UP EVERY SINGLE DAY. Sometimes you see them coming—sometimes you don't. But a few simple tricks can go a long way toward saving cash and staying healthy. Here we'll tackle food, bedbugs, more food, and even dirty underwear.

- ◎ My Embarrassing Struggle with Weight
- ◎ Why You're Still Gaining Weight on "Diet" Food
- ◎ "Sell-by" Dates: Should You Believe Them?
- ◎ Spotting Bedbugs Before They Attack
- ◎ How to Trick Your Stomach on Thanksgiving
- ◎ Don't Pay That! (Must Read If You Love Chocolate, Coffee, or Clothing)
- ◎ Used Underwear: My Most Popular Investigation . . . Ever

My Embarrassing Struggle
with Weight

It's time to open up.

I've had a long-running battle with my weight. And it's something that I think about every day. Yesterday. Today. Tomorrow. That's almost a given, I suppose, when you're in front of the camera every morning—nothing gives you "body shame" like national TV. Sometimes the camera can feel like one of those funhouse mirrors at a carnival, where suddenly you have a double chin or a beer belly.

That's all in your head, you might argue. Maybe. Except that one morning, in 2015, the *Today* show came to me and said, "Hey, we're doing a weight-loss challenge. Do you want in?"

Hint, hint.

At the time I weighed 210 pounds. With my height of six feet that meant, officially, that I was overweight. Fine . . . I was 213.

So I agreed to the Biggest Loser-esque challenge, and they put me under the wings of fitness expert Jenna Wolfe and nutritionist Joy Bauer. If you're expecting a Rocky montage where I pumped iron and did a thousand sit-ups, well, that's a very different book. Jenna gave me some useful tips that I could pull off in my hotel room. I quickly learned that the gym is not for me. I will never have shredded abs, ripped pecs, or a Channing Tatum physique.

But that's okay. I discovered that I could control my weight with food. With Joy's help, I learned that if I could drop some weight by going on a diet, then I would look better in clothes. I'd also be healthier. (Real talk: I still won't look that great with my clothes off, but hey, that doesn't matter for anyone on the planet except one person, and she's stuck with me. *Mwahahahahaha.*)

Joy put me on a strict diet: Egg whites or oatmeal in the morning. A salad for lunch. If I need to eat a sandwich, that's okay, but now I would remove the top layer of bread. It's one of my favorite tricks. Believe it or not, you won't miss that top layer. We really only eat both layers because sandwiches come that way, and they're easier to hold. So, your fingers may touch some lettuce. Big deal. Why double the carbs and the calories? At dinner I ate mostly greens and lean protein—roast chicken, fish, tuna—that kind of thing.

This doesn't mean I turned into some nutrition guru who treats my body like a holy temple. *Ha!* I'll enjoy the occasional cheat meal, I'll splurge on a burrito, and I'll even sample my share of desserts. But Joy taught me three key lessons: portion control, portion control, portion control.

For example, a friend and I were in the mood for ice cream. I craved my favorite flavor, mint chocolate chip, so I gave in to the demons and I bought a cone.

I took a bite. *Delicious.* A second. *Heaven.* I savored the cold cream, the dark bite of the chocolate, the way it felt on my tongue. A third bite. *Oh my God this is so good.* Fourth bite.

And then I threw it in the trash.

"What the hell?!" my friend said.

Here's the thing: I knew that eventually, sooner or later, I would be sad when I finished that ice cream. I would want more. You always want more. I would be sad after I ate the entire ice cream cone, I would be sad after I ate *two* ice cream cones, and I would be sad after eating just four bites. If I'm going to be sad no matter what, then why not just get it over with? I still enjoyed the experience of that sublime mint chocolate chip, as the taste lingered in my mouth for the next fifteen minutes—it pressed the pleasure button. Yet I only consumed a tiny fraction of the total calories.

Thanks to this kind of mind-set, I went from 213 pounds in 2015 to my current weight of 185.

No gimmicks. No stunts. Just good old-fashioned dieting and portion control.

I weigh myself every morning. I see the ups and downs. And sometimes I feel the judgment, like at an airport in Atlanta, when a woman saw me eating a slice of pizza and said with a *tsk-tsk*, "You're going to put that weight back on." I'm assuming she saw my weight-loss challenge on TV. If not . . . mind your own business, lady!

Sigh.

But maybe she's right? If I'm not careful, I *will* put the weight back on. So it's something that's always top of mind. I monitor my food intake. Like millions of Americans, I read the labels closely.

I depend on these labels. I trust these labels.

So if these labels might be *wrong*? You're damn right I'm going to investigate. . . .

Why You're Still Gaining Weight on "Diet" Food

I count on things like "diet desserts." (And now you know why.) Millions of Americans do. We buy the lower-calorie ice cream as a way to sneak in treats without gaining the weight. They sell low-cal ice cream, low-cal ice pops, low-cal fro-yo.

As nutritionist Joy Bauer tells me, the whole *point* of buying these diet products is because you're counting calories. And the counts should be accurate. Otherwise, what good are they? "I'd like to see the calories right on the money. But if you had a little bit of wiggle room, I'd say, no more than ten percent."

"So it should be ten percent off, tops?" I clarify.

"Tops, ten percent."

We'll see about that.

My team goes binge shopping on diet desserts, scooping up the frozen goodies like ice pops and chocolate sundaes, including one ice cream that promised just 150 calories for an entire creamy pint.

We put each sample in specially marked containers for a blind test, pack them in dry ice, and then send them to a top food laboratory. Scientists carefully measure each one. They test for calories.

The Good:

Three of the products actually have *fewer* calories than the label claimed.

The Bad:

Two of them have a bit more calories, but they were within the acceptable 10 percent threshold.

The Ugly:

Then we have the biggest losers. Take one of the desserts, a giant chocolate sundae cone, which clocks in at 13 percent more calories than the label, and the same company's ice-cream candy bar, which comes in at 16 percent more. (When contacted, the company told us that it does "rigorous testing" to make sure the labels are accurate.)

The crazy thing? Getting the calories wrong is *completely legal.* Under FDA regulations, packaged foods can vary by as much as 20 percent.

"They know they can get away with it, because the FDA allows up to twenty percent wiggle room," says Joy. "So, you know, they push the envelope a little bit. . . . It's upsetting, but it's legal."

How about a new ice cream, which somehow promises only 150 calories for an entire pint? It almost seems too good to be true.

And maybe it is. Our scientists find that one sample of the vanilla maple flavor has a whopping 46 percent more calories than advertised on the label. And the chocolate peanut butter? An incredible 68 *percent* more calories.

The manufacturer told us its calorie counts are accurate, so we asked to see those test results. We're still waiting.

"Shame on this company, really," says Joy. "I mean, people—they're eating the whole pint in really one sitting. You eat that every single day, listen, at the end of the week, you have to walk an extra nine miles just to burn off those calories."

Okay, but that's just for diet *desserts*. What about frozen diet meals?

Again, we hit the grocery store and we load our cart with brands all of us recognize. Again, we put the food in unmarked bags, ensuring a fair and blind test. Again, we send the food to the certified laboratory.

And again, we get the same frustrating results.

Some come in under: A roast beef merlot, for example, has 17 percent less fat than the label. But then again, the same company's lobster cheese ravioli has 17 percent *more* fat than the label, and other brands had similar overages. A sweet and sour chicken, for example, claims a skinny 210 calories and 2 grams of fat . . . but our scientists measure 11 percent more calories and a gut-busting *350 percent more fat*. (The company told us it was "skeptical" of our results.)

"It's enough to make you cry," says Susan Roberts, Ph.D., a leading food scientist at Tufts University. "I mean, this is disgraceful."

She should know. Dr. Roberts did similar testing in her lab and, like us, she found inaccurate labels.

"We hear all the time that people are not losing weight," says Dr. Roberts. "They're plateauing. They can't understand why they're eating almost nothing and not losing weight. Here's one explanation."

We asked the FDA to explain how this could happen, but they declined our request for an interview. A group representing the food companies, the Grocery Manufacturers Association, says that the stated numbers are merely *averages*, and that each unit of the food will vary. "The idea here is that if you see 230 calories . . . some are going to be more, some are going to be less," said a spokesperson for the Grocery Manufacturers Association.

"So you're saying it's *okay* for one particular sample to be three times higher than it says, another sample to be three times lower, as long as it averages out?" I ask.

"Well . . . that's a fact of nature. It's a matter of being practical."

Tell that to the poor customer who ends up with sweet and sour chicken, packed with *three and a half times more fat* than she expected. Tell that to the millions of Americans who depend on these labels. Tell that to the guy who lost twenty-five pounds and works hard to keep it off. Tell that to your friend who struggles with obesity. Tell that to the guy who's worried about diabetes. Tell that to your family.

"Sell-by" Dates: Should You Believe Them?

There are a few primal signals that all of us have known since childhood: Red light means stop, green light means go, and if your food is older than its "sell-by date," then you should immediately chuck it in the trash. It's second nature. It's instinctual.

And it's also dead wrong.

These dates (usually) have very little to do with safety, but are instead conjured up by the manufacturer for "peak freshness." They're trying to get you to buy more milk. And more cereal, more applesauce, and more crackers and more everything.

Let's start with eggs. They should last in your fridge and taste delicious and remain perfectly safe for *three to five weeks* after you've bought them, experts say, regardless of the date that's stamped on the carton. Still feeling squeamish? There's a cool little trick. Grab a bowl, fill it up with water, and then plop an egg into the bowl. If it drops to the bottom, that means you're good to go. If it floats to the top, go get yourself some fresh eggs.

How about dry goods, like cereals and crackers? In general, they're good for *nine to twelve months,* whether opened or unopened. Yes, it's true that after a full year they might not taste as crisp as they did originally—they might be stale, they might be extra crunchy, and they might get you some judgey stares if you serve them at a dinner party—but they're not going to make you vomit. The issue is one of taste, not health, and the food companies know it.

Or take mayonnaise. We have it drubbed into our heads that we're going to get nauseous from old mayonnaise, but a jar of mayonnaise is good for *a year and a half* unopened, and it will last for two to three months even if it's opened. Mustard lasts even longer. It angers me that the FDA hasn't cracked down on the issue. Why are these confusing dates still allowed?

There's one key exception to this rule, and that's baby formula. It's the one date that the FDA does regulate. Obviously, there's a lot on the line with babies. Using formula after the date on the bottle might not make your baby sick, per se, but it will start losing its nutritional value.

I've conducted so many interviews with folks on the street, and I've found that most people simply have no clue how little those dates matter. I'd guesstimate that, say, only 7 percent of the population is aware of this. We consume food every day, we open our fridge every day, we throw stuff away every day; this is such a huge chunk of our lives, and yet we're getting duped by the food industry.

They have brainwashed us to throw everything out long before it's truly a hazard to our health. It's baffling. People do dangerous things all the time—from driving too fast or drinking too much or smoking cigarettes—but when it comes to possibly getting a tummy ache, we freak out and use an overabundance of caution.

I'm still guilty. Even *after* I've done research on this subject and even *after* I've hosted these segments for the *Today* show, I still fall into the same trap as everyone else. That's how deeply we're programmed. Recently, my wife took some salami from the fridge, and before eating it I checked the "best by" date—a few days earlier.

"That's disgusting!" I said, and I chucked the salami in the trash.

"Didn't you debunk this?!" my wife asked, incredulous, and then she grabbed the salami out of the trash. Yes, the secret is out, my family literally goes Dumpster diving for food. We ate the salami.

And it was delicious.

185

Spotting Bedbugs Before They Attack

They're evil, gross, sneaky, and they can come from anywhere: Bedbugs. In New York City, a bedbug invasion infested a movie theater. (Who knew watching a chick flick could be so itchy?) In Connecticut, bedbugs climbed the pole inside a firehouse; in Pennsylvania, bedbugs slithered their way into a classroom; and in Colorado, the bedbugs looked to study up in a library. Not to mention outbreaks in popular retail stores.

I'll be honest, bedbugs freak me out. I'm guessing they freak you out, too. (See, I've learned from those fortune-tellers.) I hate that they are something that I can't see, can't fix, can't control. I hate that it takes forever to get rid of them.

If it seems like bedbugs are more common than they used to be, well, that's actually the case. "That's real, there are more," says Missy Henriksen, who worked for the National Pest Management Association. "One [reason] is travel, increased international travel. Also, people are getting out and enjoying the world more." We can't win, right? When society gets to a point when people want to go out and enjoy the world, we're punished with bedbugs. And, as everyone unlucky enough to get bedbugs knows, if they invade your home it can mean a whopping extermination bill, the never-ending cleaning (or torching) of old clothes, bedding, and even furniture, and *weeks* of hassle.

So here's how to spot 'em.

When climbing into a hotel bed, inspect it carefully. "You're looking for three things," explains Henriksen. "You're looking for the bug itself—a small appleseed-looking bug. You're looking for blood droplets that would be on the bed, [which is] evidence that they've been feeding on a human." (Grossed out yet?) "And you're also looking for pepper-like flakes, which is evidence of their droppings or leave behinds."

You then want to pull back the sheets, pull back the bed linens, and inspect the mattress and the mattress cover. Look for "small brown bugs" and the "droplets." Okay, some real talk: This is tricky to do, especially if the hotel bedspread is dark or brown, so Henriksen says to pay special attention to the white fabric. "You definitely have a better chance of seeing them there."

And now for the bad news: Just because the bedbugs are not in the hotel *bed* does not, necessarily, mean you're in the clear. "Unfortunately, the word bedbug is a misnomer," says Henriksen. "They can also be in picture frames, electrical sockets, your furniture, your clothes—lots of other places."

Awesome. Given that, Henriksen suggests that if there's a bedbug outbreak near you and you want to be extra vigilant, it's important to "check your clothes, check yourself when you get back home." If, for example, you go to a movie theater that has recently hosted some bedbugs, then just to be on the safe side, immediately put your clothes in the washer and "wash at a hot temperature."

Worst-case scenario: What if you spot the bedbugs at home?

Two words of advice: **Act. Now.** "The females can reproduce up to 400 offspring," explains Henriksen. "The sooner you get to the infestation, the better. The only way to properly deal with these is a trained and licensed professional; these are tough bugs to eliminate."

Four hundred offspring—wow. And I thought my three kids were a handful.

How to Trick Your Stomach
on Thanksgiving

My Thanksgiving probably looks a lot like your Thanksgiving. Every year my mom insists on cooking—no one objects; her food is amazing—and we invite our sprawling family: my brother, his wife and kids, my cousins, and the entire Rossen clan. We spend all day feasting and laughing and then feasting some more.

Throughout the day, I tend to casually stroll through the kitchen and graze on the platters of food—a spoonful of stuffing here, a forkful of yams there. I never give it much thought. Sometimes, in horrifying moments of clarity, I do notice how much food I consume on my plate at dinner, but I rarely do a full reckoning of all the calories inhaled on this glorious day of gluttony.

The bad news is that I'm blissfully unaware of how much I really eat. The good news? Experts say you can trick your brain to consume *less* food on Thanksgiving. A lot less. And you don't have to go hungry, go on a diet, stop eating carbs, or deny yourself even one bite of mom's delicious green bean casserole. You'll feel full.

To see if it's really possible to trick your brain, my team cooked up a little experiment. Meet the Clendennys. They're a big, all-American family that we treated to an early Thanksgiving dinner. (Note: We're not monsters. We didn't want to ruin their *actual* holiday, so we set up a "pre-Thanksgiving" meal two weeks in advance, cooking turkey and stuffing and mac and cheese—we simulated everything short of asking the Lions and the Cowboys to play an extra game of football.)

We feed the Clendennys ham, mashed potatoes, dressing—the works. We do not instruct anyone to eat more or less than usual. We do not tell them to eat slowly or quickly. We let them do their own thing at their own pace.

Yet I have a few tricks up my sleeve. We split the Clendennys into two equal-sized groups.

Group 1: We serve the trays of food directly on their table. Those heaping piles of food—the Himalayas of Carbs—are all within easy reach. This is how my family eats. This is how most families eat. They drink white wine and they use white plates.

Group 2: Here, we mix it up. This wing of the Clendenny family has to get up from their seats and serve themselves from a buffet. An even more important difference? The buffet has multiple courses. At the start of dinner, the buffet offers a spread of vegetables, salad, and other healthy options. Then, in the second course, they could devour the ham and stuffing and potatoes to their hearts' content. They drink red wine and they use blue plates.

We set up the experiment . . . *Go!*

"I'm so hungry!" one Clendenny exclaims, digging into her food.

"Let's eat!"

"Everything looks delicious!"

"Wow!"

They eat in two different rooms of the same house, so I can walk back and forth and monitor their progress, trying not to be too jealous of all their stuffing and turkey. (Alas, I couldn't find a way to sneak "Jeff Rossen eats all the food he can, without gaining a pound!" into this particular experiment.) Both groups keep eating and laughing and piling on more food. Both groups keep marveling at how good it tastes. Both groups thank us.

But here's what they don't know.

While the Clendennys scarfed up the spoils of Thanksgiving, we brought in a nutrition expert, Keri Glassman, who weighed the food beforehand so she could keep track of how much each group ate. She jotted down every calorie.

"Did you see the group eating family style?" she asks me. "They're going to town. It's carb central. They are loading up, because it's right in front of them."

She furiously punches numbers into a calculator. After this frenzy of food math, she shows me the total calories consumed by Group 2 (the buffet group, eating on blue plates and drinking red wine): 9,218 calories. Not bad. That's a respectable amount of calories!

But now let's look at Group 1. This is the table that ate more "like normal," with the food served directly on the table. They ate on white plates. Their total: 14,632. Whoa. That's a whopping increase of 59 percent. It's a game changer.

Oh, and how about the wine? We kept track of that, too. Group 2 (drinking red wine) drank two bottles. Group 1 (drinking white) drank *six* bottles.

A few things explain this massive difference. At the start of the meal, Group 2 loaded up on the salad and roasted vegetables, so that when it was time for that second trip to the buffet—where they scooped up the ham and the stuffing—they were less likely to overindulge. They got that initial rush to eat out of their system, on greens.

And the blue plates actually make a difference. "Blue is traditionally an unappetizing color," says Keri. "When we eat on blue plates or we dine in a blue room, research has even shown that we eat less."

Color matters with the wine, too. "When you pour white wine, you often pour more, because there's no contrast with the glass. So you pour with a heavier hand," Keri explains. You can see red against the glass better. So the glass looks fuller. It's subconscious but it's real. "So if you want to cut back this Thanksgiving, go for the red over the white."

The great news here? None of these tricks involve a sacrifice. Both groups told us they were full!

You can tweak a few simple things in the *presentation* of your food, and then eat like normal.

The even greater news? All of these lessons apply to *all* meals, during all months of the year, not just Thanksgiving. This could add up to serious weight loss. Who knew?

Don't Pay That! (A Must-Read If You Love Chocolate, Coffee, or Clothing)

I'm not a big fan of wasting money. I guess I should thank my parents for this mind-set, as my mom was a high-school math teacher and my dad was a dentist. We lived comfortably but not lavishly. Take our vacations, for example. My parents saved up so that once every three or four years—about as often as the Summer Olympics—the whole family could get on a plane and travel to someplace like Disney World. That vacation felt like the biggest deal in the world . . . and it was. We all stayed in one room at the Holiday Inn—my brother and my mom and my dad—squeezing into two queen beds. Saving money is part of what makes me tick.

So if I could buy Product A for $5 and Product B for $10, and I can't tell the difference between Product A and Product B, why on earth would I throw away money on Product B?

Yet we do it all the time. Almost all of us, every day, chuck away money without thinking. Let's take just three examples: clothing, coffee, and chocolate. (The 3 Cs)

CLOTHING

It used to be that when you bought a cheap suit, it looked rumpled or boxy or gangly or like "dad's old suit." Not anymore. The cheaper stuff can look just as good as the Armanis and Zegnas of the world.

Contrary to popular belief, the stuff in the outlets isn't just the leftover dregs from the main store. There's great stuff there. So, for many of us looking for a good deal, a lot of the big-name retailers have created outfits with similar looks for less, made specifically for their outlet stores. Maybe the stitching isn't as detailed or the fabric isn't as fancy, but your friends, family, and coworkers probably can't tell the difference.

Need proof?

We set up an experiment to see whether the average person could tell the difference between the expensive brands and the discounted clothes from outlet stores. "For the naked eye, between retail and outlet, [people] can't tell," says Aly Scott, professional stylist and founder of StyleChic.

She sets up a table with two identical-looking piles of clothing: some denim shirts and cotton T-shirts. One is retail and costs $206, one is from the outlet and costs $111. I stare at them both, unaware which is which.

I run my hands over the cotton and denim, trying to channel my inner designer. (I bet my oldest daughter would do better at this.) "This one feels a little more *structured*," I say, basically making up fashiony-sounding words, "and this one feels heavier. I'm going with this one being the more expensive one." I point to the one on the left.

"Incorrect."

Okay, so clearly *I* couldn't tell the difference between an expensive outfit and the cheaper alternative, but what about savvy New Yorkers who are more fashion conscious than I am? (In other words: everyone.)

We style two of our producers, Kathryn and Jovanna, in identical-looking outfits that include white shirts and navy jackets. Kathryn's outfit, head to toe, costs $289 from the J. Crew outlet store. Jovanna went to the regular J. Crew and forked over $660—more than double.

As the two ladies stroll through the streets of New York, patiently posing and even spinning around, we ask people to guess which outfit costs more money. Some get it right. But most get it wrong.

"You're kidding me!" one guy says, amazed that Kathryn's outfit is cheaper.

"The one on the right?" one woman guesses . . . and gets it wrong.

But what about accessories? We buy Coach wallets. One's from the Coach outlet ($107), one's from the Coach retail store ($272). "I do like the detail," says one woman of our Coach outlet wallet, thinking it was more expensive. "I like the zipper. It makes a difference to me."

"Guess what?" I say. "Wrong. You like the cheaper one."

She laughs. "Does that mean I can have it?"

And for the grand finale, on the *Today* show stage I show up in my gray suit . . . and I'm joined by a very special guest, my producer Josh, dressed in an identical-looking suit. We have the same light gray suits, same blue-striped ties, same brown shoes. (Josh, though, has a far wider smile—he's eating this up.)

One of the suits is $923. The other costs around $369, head to toe. Matt Lauer and Savannah Guthrie both look at us, taking in the sartorial splendor. Which one costs more?

Both of them touch our sleeves and our arms, brushing the fabric with their fingers. Not weird at all.

"I think this is the more expensive one," says Matt, pointing to Josh.

"I agree," says Savannah.

Nope! I reveal that Josh is wearing the outlet version.

"No way!" says Savannah.

"It's much softer!" gushes Matt, again feeling the fabric of Josh's outlet suit, incredulous. (And for what it's worth, he's the best-dressed guy I know. Matt even worked in a men's clothing store for years. The man knows his threads.)

Moral of the story: You don't have to break the bank to look like a million bucks.

COFFEE

We're all obsessed with our morning coffee. I know I am. For years, without even really thinking about it, I plunked down three dollars every morning for my name-brand coffee, treating myself to this little indulgence.

That was part of my morning routine. And routines are most rigid in the morning, right? Think about it. At night there are a million different curveballs—dinner plans, errands, a social engagement, a soccer game for your kid—but every morning begins the same way. My alarm buzzes at 5:05 A.M., I'm in the shower by 5:17, I'm out of the house at 6:05, and I have my three-dollar coffee in hand by 6:37. Clockwork.

The only problem? That routine costs some serious cash. The average American spends over *$1,000 a year* on coffee, mainly because we don't even think about it, and we're convinced that we need "the good stuff" as opposed to a thriftier alternative, like the cups of joe they sell at the deli for one dollar.

But can you tell the difference?

At a shopping mall in Edison, New Jersey, I transform myself into the world's nosiest barista, setting up a coffee experiment. I pour two different types of coffee: One is the "gourmet" stuff from a fancy shop that costs three dollars a cup. (Technically $3.25.) The other is the humble cup of coffee you get from the deli—one buck, flat.

As the curious mall shoppers approach my pop-up coffee stand, I pour the hot coffee into unmarked cups, so they don't know whether they're drinking the gourmet or the cheapo. They drink both varieties and have to pick which one they like best.

One guy sips a cup of coffee, thinks hard, and says, "That one's got a better, smoother flavor."

He didn't know he had just picked the one-dollar deli coffee.

"I like this one," says one woman, unwittingly pointing at the cheap stuff.

"I like this one better," says another, also choosing the humble deli coffee.

In fact, amazingly, *67 percent* preferred the cheap deli coffee. Yet we spend so much on the gourmet! It's bonkers when you think about it. After this experiment, I changed my behavior and now, every morning, I grab a one-dollar coffee from the deli. And guess what? It's my new routine.

CHOCOLATE

Okay, by now you can see where this is going, and yes, you are right. I head back to the mall and bring two different brands of chocolate: generic milk chocolate that costs 16 cents apiece, and gourmet milk chocolate that's *five times* more expensive—81 cents apiece.

This time I actually blindfold the contestants. We have them try the cheap stuff and the fancy stuff, and we give them crackers and water as a palette cleanser.

"It's, like, creamier," says one woman about the *fancy* chocolate.

"It's creamier," says another woman about the *cheap* chocolate.

One says that the cheap chocolate "just has a little more flavor to it."

The results? About fifty-fifty. Nearly half said they liked the cheaper chocolate better. And it turns out there's a reason. "It's got more sugar, it's sweeter," says chocolate expert Liz Gutman, referring to the cheaper stuff. (Aside: I love that there are "chocolate experts." How do I get that job?) "That's what people are used to. That's what they grew up eating."

She says that it's true that expensive chocolates have finer ingredients and more cocoa but, just like with coffee, if your taste buds can't tell the difference, why fork over the extra dough?

So clothing, coffee, and chocolate? Buy cheap. You're welcome.

Used Underwear: My Most Popular Investigation . . . Ever

I'm sitting in an executive conference room at NBC World Headquarters in New York City.

I'm wearing a suit. I take a deep breath, and I try to make strong, confident eye contact with some of the most senior people at the network.

"I want to buy women's underwear," I say, "and then take the underwear home. And then I'll return the underwear, and see if stores are reselling them."

Silence.

Okay, maybe I should back up. Awhile back I was with my wife, shopping for clothes. She picked up some underwear and showed them to me.

"I've always wondered if someone else tried these on before," she said.

"You mean, wore them and then *returned* them?" I asked, incredulous.

"Who knows what these clerks are doing, and if they're putting it back on the rack?"

She didn't know if it happened. And *I* certainly didn't know. Then I realized that almost *no one* knew if customers could buy a pair of underwear, return it . . . only for the stores to slap a tag on it and resell it as new.

Back in 2010, I met a woman named Tiffany Luxinger, who told me this happens all the time. Okay, but what does she know? Well . . . she had worked at *three* different Victoria's Secret stores, and she pulled no punches. "If a product comes back as returned, it obviously has an odor to it," Tiffany told me. "We will put it on a hanger, hang it up to dry overnight so the odor has time to come out of the product. We'll retag it . . . and put it back on the sales floor."

Wait, WTF? I couldn't believe what I was hearing. Were these just a few rogue Victoria's Secret stores, or was the problem widespread? This is why I humiliated myself in front of the execs at 30 Rock. We would deploy hidden cameras and hunt for the truth, no matter where the journey took us. (Your move, Woodward and Bernstein.)

Across a variety of retail stores—Victoria's Secret, the Gap, Macy's, etc.—my team bought underwear and bikinis, pulled out the protective stripping (to make it look like it had been worn), and then marked the tags with two tiny black dots, which would later help us identify the undies.

A week later we headed back to these same stores, returning the goods.

"Hi. I'd just like to return this stuff," said my producer with a smile. At Bloomingdale's, to my amazement and horror, the clerk retagged the underwear, then casually walked it back to the sales racks to sell them as new. Same with Victoria's Secret. At the Gap they moved even faster—they tried to resell the underwear *within seconds*, practically right before our very eyes.

Incredibly, it's not technically "illegal" to sell used underwear, but it could have health implications. "Fecal material would be the most concerning substance," says microbiologist Peter Kmieck, in case you weren't already grossed out. "You could have bacteria, viruses, fungi. These are things that one person would be able to transfer to another inadvertently through the garment."

That didn't stop most stores. Give some credit to J. Crew, Saks Fifth Avenue, and Express—none of them tried to resell the used knickers. But at Macy's and Nordstrom? Different story. At Nordstrom, they took our bikini and gave it new tags . . . even though it had no hygienic liner. (We had ripped it off.) At Macy's we found our underwear back on the sales rack retagged like new.

Tiffany Luxinger, the woman who had worked at three different Victoria's Secrets, told us that, at times, the managers would pressure them to push as much merchandise back to the floor as soon as possible, "so we could make more money."

"Did stained items end up back on the sales floor?" I asked her.

"Yes. The employees, they're in a rush, a lot of them don't care and they don't double-check to make sure that it was used or not."

Okay. It was time to take it up a notch. For the next round, before returning the goods, we *visibly stained* several pairs of underwear with baby oil. Surely no store would take back underwear stained with baby oil, right?

Wrong.

At the Gap, Bloomingdale's, Victoria's Secret, and Macy's, they not only took back the stained panties, but they put them back out for sale. Let me repeat that. These companies accepted used underwear that was stained with baby oil, then they gave it a new tag, then tried to sell it at full price to someone like you. (Quick aside: They never actually succeeded at reselling *these* particular pairs of underwear, as our producers worked undercover to ensure no poor customer actually bought the spoiled goods. But if we hadn't been there . . .)

We reached out to all of these companies, and all of them told us that customers' safety and satisfaction are top concerns and their employees made a mistake in reselling used merchandise. They said that our investigation has prompted them to "reeducate" their workers about the policy.

"Reeducate." Hmmm. Did the reeducation work?

A few months later we tested again. Just like before, our intrepid producers went undercover and bought some panties and bras and bikinis, took them home, and marked each pair with two tiny black dots. They even stained several with baby oil again. A week later we returned them.

"Hi. I'd like to return these," said our producer at Victoria's Secret.

The clerk inspected the panties. "We can't take panties back that have the tags removed, because it's an underwear, and the tags are removed."

"Oh," said our producer, pretending to be disappointed.

"So it's, like a health hazard," said the Victoria's Secret clerk.

Yes! I gave a little fist pump. Good job, Victoria's Secret. Next, we headed to Nordstrom to see if they had learned anything. Our producer tried to return her underwear but, perhaps because of our story, it ended up in a plastic bag.

"Why did you put it in a plastic bag?" asked our producer.

"Because the tag is removed," said the clerk. "I can't sell this back."

Yes.

We go to the Gap: They, too, refused to resell it.

Macy's: same.

Bloomingdales: same.

Well, hot damn. When these stores told us they would reeducate their employees and enforce the policy, it looked like they actually meant it. It's not often in life that I can see clear, concrete results. Mission accomplished. Victory.

. . . Or was it? Fast-forward four years. The retailers had managed to change their behavior for a few months, but did it really stick? Viewers kept e-mailing me about the story for weeks, months, and then years, so I felt that I owed the nation one final update.

"It's the grossest story you have ever done," Savannah Guthrie told me, and she's not wrong. So we retested the same stores as before—Victoria's Secret, Nordstrom, Macy's, Bloomingdale's, and the Gap.

We head to Bloomingdale's and perform our now-familiar routine. The clerk takes the underwear to the back room. . . . and the panties are never seen again. Good job, Bloomingdale's.

Nordstrom: clean.

The Gap: clean.

Macy's: clean.

So far, so good. Then, however, we return to the original scene of the crime, Victoria's Secret, where that former employee had told us that they would actually hang the used underwear overnight to "remove the odor."

We return two pairs of underwear to Victoria's Secret. The cashier quickly tosses them behind her . . . and soon they're back on the for-sale table, with new tags, and we can see our two tiny black dots as proof. Busted.

So, of course, the usual statement rolled in. Victoria's Secret told us that what we discovered is a clear violation of their policy, promising to "reeducate" its staff. But we've heard that before.

Hey, retailers? Sometimes I forget what I had for breakfast, but sometimes I have a long, looooooong memory. And I'm still on the case.

See you in 2023.

8

BET YOU DIDN'T KNOW . . .

WHO KNEW THAT MEN AND women often pay different prices for the *exact same product?* Or that dousing a fire with water can actually make things *worse?* Bet you didn't know . . .

- ⊚ The Pink Tax: How Women Pay More for the Same Stuff
- ⊚ How to Survive a Heart Attack
- ⊚ Shred It or Save It?
- ⊚ How to Stop Your Kitchen from Burning Down
- ⊚ Three of My Favorite Shopping Tricks
- ⊚ Your Fake Fur Isn't Really Fake

The Pink Tax: How Women Pay More for the Same Stuff

I'm writing to you from inside a bubble. The Man Bubble. Like most men, I walk through life unaware of the many injustices, big and small, that confront women: the subtle (and not so subtle) forms of sexism, the gender pay gap, the male gaze, the pain of childbirth, body shaming, and the list goes on and on. The deck is often stacked against women. (One exception: rain boots. Women have a much wider selection of rain boots.)

The point is that in the Man Bubble, we tend not to notice these discrepancies. And I sure didn't think that gender discrimination would be so blatant, so in-your-face, that women would pay more for the very same product . . . just because it's pink.

But they do. Women pay a Pink Tax.

"It's everything from deodorant to razors and shaving cream," retail expert Andrea Woroch tells me.

"I've never noticed this," I say.

"You *wouldn't* notice this, because women's products are separated from the men's products," says Andrea. "So it's not easy to compare the prices."

I had never really thought about that. Almost *no one* thinks about that, because women shop in the "pink" aisles, men shop in the "blue" aisles, and never the two shall meet (metaphorically speaking). To see this in action, I go on a shopping trip with my producer Jovanna and we hit a large store to buy exactly the same products from exactly the same brands—the only difference is that hers are pink, mine are blue.

I pick up a bottle of men's shaving gel: $2.29.

Jovanna grabs the exact same brand with nearly identical packaging, but pink: $2.39. She pays an extra dime, simply because she's a woman.

Okay, how about shampoo? I grab a bottle of men's two-in-one shampoo and conditioner: $3.99.

From the pink section, Jovanna reaches for the exact same brand. Women's two-in-one shampoo and conditioner: $4.79.

But why?

The company told us prices can vary and as for the men's and women's two-in-one hair products, they have different formulas and the women's ingredients cost more.

C'mon, *how is that possible?* I look at the bottles closer. To my untrained eyes, it sure looks like they have the same active ingredients.

In fact, our retail expert Andrea says what's really going on here is this: "Brands know that women will pay more to look good and feel good. And, by targeting these products specifically to women, they know they'll pick those up."

"And you do," I say.

"And we do."

Next, we head to deodorant. A popular deodorant for men: $3.89.

The same brand's deodorant for women: $4.89.

Sometimes it's even more egregious. In the same aisle I spot a "twin pack" of another popular men's deodorant, and that one costs $4.79. Not a bad deal. But for women, their twin pack costs $8.79, nearly *twice as much* as what I pay. It doesn't seem fair. We reached out to the maker of all the deodorants, who told us the only reason for the price difference is because the deodorants come from different product lines with different technologies. Draw your own conclusions . . .

The Pink Tax, I soon learn, extends far beyond the shopping

cart. Take the dry cleaner, for example. Jovanna and I drop off two shirts to the same dry cleaner and compare the cost. I bring a standard white button-down. Jovanna drops off a woman's blouse that's basically the same thing. (Confession: I'm still not totally sure on the distinction between a "shirt" and a "blouse." Maybe that will be a future Rossen Report.)

My bill for the shirt? $2.50.

Jovanna's bill for the blouse? $5.00. Once again, twice as much. And this is all from just *one day* of errands. Now, think about *all* the trips to the stores and the cleaners. Experts say that when you crunch the numbers and do the math, women are paying nearly $1,400 more a year . . . just by buying products targeted to them. It's so unfair. And now I'm surprised that they don't make "women's toothpaste" (in a nice pink box) or "women's dental floss" or even "women's contact lenses."

Here's the best advice for women: Come join us inside the Man Bubble. Experts say our cheaper products work just as well for women, too, and will save you money.

How to Survive a Heart Attack

When you're in your twenties or thirties, you never really think much about heart attacks. Just before I turned forty, I thought that heart attacks were for people in their sixties or fifties or *maybe* mid- to late forties. . . . but not someone like me. Not someone young. Not someone healthy.

So, one day on an airplane, while sitting down, all of a sudden I couldn't catch my breath. I wasn't doing jumping jacks. I wasn't lifting weights. (You will never see me lifting weights.) I wasn't even huffing up a few flights of stairs. I was just sitting still, trying not to think about airplane germs. My breath was short. I was dizzy and sweating. I felt a *pang-pang-pang* inside my chest. I walked off the plane, scared, but then it subsided so I tried to ignore it.

Then it happened again a week later . . . *when I was sitting on the couch*. Soon I googled these symptoms—and any time you google symptoms, of course, you convince yourself you're going to die—I immediately decided I have heart issues. So I saw my doctor for a checkup. I got tests, chest X-rays, saw a cardiologist, the works. The verdict? I was healthy but I needed to drop some weight. (I was still 213 at the time.) And the real takeaway? Heart attacks can be *way more common* than you think. Plus, I'm a father. I have people who depend on me. I need to know how to save my life or someone else's.

My ignorance is fairly typical, as one study found that less than 3 percent of Americans are trained in CPR. The math gets scarier: If your heart stops and no one helps, your chance of survival is a paltry 6 percent.

Yet, there's good news. You don't need to be a paramedic or a lifeguard or officially trained in CPR, as there are some very basic things you can do to save a life. Dr. David Markenson, an emergency response advisor with the American Red Cross, boils it all down to just a few simple things to remember.

WHEN SOMEONE HAS A HEART ATTACK:
"The first thing you should do is call 911," says Dr. Markenson. "Emergency help will then be on its way."

The second step: aspirin. "It's the most important thing in a heart attack you can do to save a life," says Markenson. "It helps keep blood pumping to the heart."

Wait, but let's be a bit realistic. When someone is having a heart attack it's really, really scary and they are not, usually, in a state where they will calmly open their mouth and pop an aspirin. So do you force-feed it? Short answer—yes. "If they're awake and they can swallow, give them the aspirin to save their life," says Markenson.

If their heart actually stops, then they're now in cardiac arrest, and as Markenson says, "the most important thing is an AED," or automated external defibrillator. You might be saying to yourself, *You know what, I generally don't just happen to have an automated external defibrillator with me whenever I leave the home.* Yet they're everywhere, almost hiding in plain sight.

"Most places . . . like 30 Rock have one, but most people don't know where they are," Markenson tells me.

"Let me tell you, I think I know where ours is here at NBC," I say, maybe a little too smugly.

"Can you show me where your AED is?" he asks.

Uh-oh.

"I think . . . I think it's this way."

Crap. Where is the damn thing? I lead him down one hallway, where I think I saw the AED hanging on a wall—or was it under a counter? Then we change directions and I lead him down a different hallway.

"It's in here, right?" I say. But it's not.

I check another room, another hallway, another closet.

"Is it in here?" Nope.

Finally I locate the AED near the elevator—"Got it!" I tell Dr. Markenson proudly. "How long was that?"

He had been timing me. One minute and forty-three seconds. "That was way too long," says Markenson, disappointed. The victim could have died.

(Speaking of which, do you know where the AED is at your job? I bet your company has one. Find it. This will spare you some embarrassment if Dr. Markenson ever comes to give you a pop quiz and, more importantly, it could save a life.)

"Anyone can use an AED," says Markenson. "It gives you step-by-step instructions." I'm not going to give you blow-by-blow instructions of how to use the AED right here because, let's be honest, you're not going to remember. But it's important that you do remember this key takeaway:

You can use an AED, and all you have to do is follow the simple instructions printed right on the machine.

Many of them even come with a computerized voice that talks you through it in real time. Plus, most AEDs have photos printed on them so you can see where to put the pads.

I'll confess, though, part of me was still a little freaked out by the idea of placing electric pads on a person's chest and sending shockwaves through their body. I mean, I'm not a doctor. What if I do it wrong? What if I accidentally electrocute some poor old man who wasn't really having a heart attack, but was just burping?

Happily, the clever makers of the AED thought of this very issue, and they gave it a cool additional feature: It's impossible to "accidentally" shock someone. When you put the pads on their chest, the machine instantly analyzes the patient and determines whether they need a shock or not.

And what if this happens to someone and you're outside, and there's no AED around?

"CPR is the key thing," advises Dr. Markenson. "If they're unresponsive and not breathing, just push hard and fast, center of the chest."

You might be thinking, okay, but I'm not totally sure how to do that. So there are some final things to keep in mind:

1) You can download the Red Cross First Aid app, so the instructions are right on your phone if someone has a heart attack. I have this app and it gives me peace of mind.

2) And maybe most importantly—don't just stand there idly. Even a crude *attempt* of CPR is more effective than just watching. "It's not even important to be perfect," says Markenson. "Doing something is better than doing nothing." And that's not a bad mantra for all life-and-death situations: *Doing something is better than nothing.*

Shred It or Save It?

Should you shred or save your old paper files?

This issue has baffled me for years, as the advice always seems so back and forth. On the one hand, we're taught that, as responsible citizens and shoppers, we should keep our paperwork handy for future reference. On the other hand, I don't want to be a hoarder. So . . . which is it? Who can keep it all straight?

Luckily, you bought this book. After consulting with the experts, I have your dead-simple guide for how to handle each document:

Tax return: *Save* it. But only for three years, as that's the recommendation from the IRS. Then save it forever as a digital copy.

Store receipts: *Shred* it. You might *think* you need these for when you file taxes, but the IRS says that for anything under $75, don't even bother. You only need to keep receipts for big-ticket items or in case they include the actual warranty.

Pay stub: *Shred* it. You don't need 'em. Once you check to make sure your pay is accurate, you can (and should) shred them, as most employers keep a copy of this stuff online.

Last will and testament: *Save* it. You want to keep this baby in a safe place. And tell friends and relatives where you keep it, just in case.

Bank statement: *Shred* it. Just like with pay slips, you only need to look at these things once to verify their accuracy, and after that, ditch 'em. If your bank doesn't keep online copies of your statements, then it probably shouldn't be your bank.

This book: *Save* it. Or else what would you do the day your plane crashes into a tornado that leaves you stranded at sea, with only a dishonest locksmith there to rescue you?

How to Stop Your Kitchen from Burning Down

Recently, my local fire department put on a big neighborhood fair—free music, free popcorn, free ice cream, free cotton candy—

the works. They lured us in with the free sugary treats, then they taught us a fire-safety lesson.

As my seven-year-old daughter, Sloane, chomped on cotton candy, she looked up to see a simulated kitchen fire. The firefighters poured water on the flames, and *whooooooosssshhh*—it grew even larger, brighter, scarier.

"Daddy, I thought that water put fire *out*?" she said.

She's not alone. From the time we played with toy fire trucks as little kids, we're taught that you extinguish a fire by dousing it with water. After all, the "fire hydrant" is connected to gushing water that's used to spray on the flames.

But not with grease fires. It turns out that most house fires start in the kitchen, and these mini-infernos kill hundreds of people every year. Grease fires are one of the leading causes. They burn hot, they spread fast and, if you're not careful, they can quickly engulf your entire home in flames.

To learn how to survive these fires, I head to the Morris County Public Safety Training Academy, in New Jersey, where Fire Captain David Hamilton shows me the ropes. He leads me to a simulated kitchen.

His first advice is simple: "Everybody needs to have a fire extinguisher in their home, and know where it is," says Captain Hamilton, a muscular, no-nonsense guy with a buzzed haircut.

Hmmm . . . I'm 100 percent confident that I have a fire extinguisher in my home, but I'm only 37 percent confident that I know exactly where it is.

KEY TAKEAWAY: Owning a fire extinguisher doesn't do you a lick of good if you can't find it in a blink. (This weekend—literally this weekend—make it a point to locate your fire extinguisher. Trust me. It's easier to do this on a calm Sunday morning than when your kitchen is on fire.)

"After finding it, you have to know how to use it," Hamilton continues. There's an easy acronym that even I can remember: PASS.

Pull the pin

Aim

Squeeze the handle

Sweep side to side

He puts an oven mitt on the stove, then lights it on fire, then hands me the fire extinguisher. It's my first time using one. I stand a couple of feet from the burning stove, pull the pin, aim it at the flames, squeeze the trigger, and then spray side to side.

Instantly the fire disappears. *Wow.* That was much easier than I had imagined.

Then he ignites something far more dangerous: a grease fire.

"If I didn't have a fire extinguisher, my first reaction would be to throw water on this," I admit, echoing my daughter.

"No, water would be the *worst* thing to put on a grease fire," says Captain Hamilton. "It would actually spread it. Let me show you an example."

He takes a cup of water, and while the two of us stand just a few feet from the stove, he splashes it on the flames. A fireball explodes from the stove, and I cover my eyes and jump back. *"Whoa!"* I say, somehow using "whoa" instead of another four-letter word.

"Okay, so what are you *supposed* to do?" I ask.

"Common household material—baking soda," says the Fire Captain, calm, as the flames continue to dance on the stove. (This guy has ice in his veins.)

"Regular baking soda?"

"Regular baking soda." (By the way, flour won't work. It needs to be baking soda.)

He hands me a box and instructs me to pour it over the flames. I sprinkle a little of the powder, almost like I'm salting popcorn, and the flames continue to burn. *Damnit. I'm doing it wrong.*

"Keep going," instructs the firefighter, still calm. "The whole box."

I swallow my fear and just dump the entire box on the flames. And within *seconds* the entire fire is snuffed. *Poof.* Gone. It's that easy. A fire extinguisher would also have worked.

As I leave the simulated kitchen, I feel strangely upbeat, even buoyant. Sometimes I leave these experiments feeling more anxiety about the world, thinking *Wow, that was more dangerous than I thought.* But sometimes I leave with a renewed sense of confidence, even optimism. While it's true that fires are scary, it is *not* true that we're powerless.

We don't need to be action heroes to use a fire extinguisher; before pulling the trigger I had expected a recoil, like from a rifle, but instead it was gentle and smooth. These fire extinguishers are built for everyday Joes like you and me. Don't let them intimidate you. All we need to do is keep our wits about us, remember some basics like PASS, think twice before spraying water (especially on a grease fire), and always stock up on the baking soda.

Three of My Favorite Shopping Tricks

I'm chronically cheap. My wife is the spender, I'm the saver. Hell, I still have my bar mitzvah money in my bank account. Through the good years and the bad, the highs and the lows, I've always thought that whatever money I have could go away tomorrow—*poof.* So I'm cautious, and I *love* the thrill of a deal.

This is why when I come home from work to a pile of Amazon Prime boxes on my doorstep—these boxes feed Danielle's online shopping habit—I almost have a daily heart attack. (Thankfully, I now know what to do in the event of a heart attack.) So I do whatever I can to steer Danielle toward deals and tips and bargains. Then everybody wins, as she gets what she wants and I get the rush of pulling one over on the stores.

This is a long-winded way of saying—okay, *confessing*—that I used the resources of the *Today* show to teach my wife a lesson. I have access to the best experts in the country, and I'm going to use it, dammit.

Here's what the experts tell me: It's possible to negotiate. I always thought that when you go shopping, you can only really haggle at Mom and Pop shops, or maybe when you're trying to buy a used banjo at the flea market. But not according to retail expert Andrea Woroch, who says you can actually save real cash at the big-box stores.

"You're saying there's a way to save big money on big-ticket items?" I ask her breathlessly, thinking of my wife.

"Yes, it's that simple. People just don't know what to do," says Andrea.

So she agrees to join me on a shopping trip and show me her money-saving magic, sharing three tips that almost no one ever uses.

TIP 1: THE PRICE MATCH

The first stop is a big-name home-improvement store. We roam the aisles and scan the endless rows of microwaves and blenders and dishwashers. Finally, Andrea settles on one dishwasher, staring at it, intense, until a salesperson comes over to help. (She's a pro.)

The salesperson asks if she needs any help.

Andrea frowns a little—remember, she's undercover—and points to the dishwasher. "I just was going to price check them against other retailers."

I'm a little nervous and uncomfortable, wondering if we've broken some shopper's code. Would the guy be insulted?

To my surprise, he doesn't miss a beat. "We do price checks," he says. The salesman hops online and finds another store selling it for forty-four dollars less. Then he agrees to slash the price.

Boom! Andrea just saved forty-four dollars. And in case not every salesperson is that proactive, you can actually do your own price checking with apps on your phone (there are plenty), like ShopSavvy, that instantly scour nearby stores for better deals. It's easy, quick, and has absolutely no downside.

Still . . . I'm skeptical . . . do apps like that *actually* work? To put it to the test, Andrea whisks me to a big-name electronics store and pretends that she wants to buy a laptop. Out pops her phone and Andrea scans in the bar code, taps her phone, and a few seconds later, she finds the same laptop at another store for ninety dollars cheaper.

"I think I found it for a better price . . ." she politely says to the salesman.

Once again, I worry he might be offended. Once again, he doesn't miss a beat.

"We'll match the price," he says with good cheer.

TIP 2: THE OPEN BOX

Andrea then hunts around the TV department until she sees what she's looking for—an item in an "open box" that has been returned. The products inside the box are often in perfectly good condition. Someone bought the item, tried it out, and then decided, for example, that they'd rather have a sixty-inch flat-screen, not the fifty-five. The TV might not have an unbroken plastic seal, but who cares? (It's not like the TV is, say, underwear.) Sometimes the item might be missing a few accessories.

Enter Andrea.

She inspects the open TV box and suggests a more creative solution. "Can you throw in, like, a free remote, or a free stand, or some kind of like additional discount [since it's missing those items]?"

The salesman thinks. He considers this unusual proposal. Then he goes to speak to his supervisor, comes back, and tells us that they'll do it . . . knocking off $280.

Mind. Blown.

TIP 3: BUNDLING

For the final stop on our Magical Savings Tour, Andrea takes me to a major appliance store. She promises to teach me the secret art of bundling: The more you buy, the more you can haggle and save.

"So I'm looking for a washer and dryer," Andrea says to the salesperson. He shows her around, she checks out the appliances, and then she says that she *also* has an eye on a refrigerator. (How many appliances does this woman need? No judgment, though.)

"If I just bought all three, just do the deal now, you can help me out?" she asks.

Again, the manager thinks. And, again, the store comes through, lopping $349 off the price.

Whoa. I've been doing it wrong all my life, and I thought *I* was a savvy shopper. One final tip? Just be nice. Experts say that employees will probably give you a better deal if you're polite.

Some of the Rossen Reports have saved lives, prevented injuries, exposed fraud, and maybe even led to social change. But that all pales compared to saving big bucks on a dishwasher. I feel so victorious. Suddenly, all of Danielle's shopping trips have now become an opportunity to save cash. Life goal: COMPLETE.

Your Fake Fur Isn't Really Fake

It's ironic. Time after time, Rossen Reports has discovered that retailers are claiming that something is real, but instead selling you a fake.

Here we have the opposite.

A recent Gallup poll found that nearly 100 million Americans think buying and wearing *real* fur is morally wrong. So some of the biggest brands have switched their tactics: Now they sell "faux fur" to let people stay warm, stylish, and free of guilt.

As one faux-fur-wearing lady told us, "I don't see the point [in] killing an animal for that kind of money [when] a fake one looks just as good, and it's warm." As another said, "We're all for the fake fur. We love it."

But it might not be fake.

To investigate, my team orders a closetful of faux-fur jackets, sweaters, and boots from a variety of major retailers. All of them proudly advertise the items as faux fur.

I pick up two of the brown fur jackets. They all feel pretty soft, and I can't tell the difference between what's real and what's fake. But that's why we have scientists. So we send the clothes to a lab in Chicago, where a team of scientists, clad in white lab coats, tests the hairs using their gadgets and microscopes.

Chris Palenik, a research microscopist, examines a faux-fur sweater, then he looks up at me. "It's actually *rabbit fur* that's been dyed."

Yep. A cute, furry, adorable rabbit has been killed, and the real fur was used in place of faux fur. We give the scientist another one to analyze, this time a big-name designer jacket bought from a department store. Weirdly, this jacket was advertised online as faux fur, but when we get the actual coat in the mail, it says "real animal fur" on the tag. So which is it?

"It's real animal fur," says Palenik. "From a coyote." The scientists also found evidence of real fur from "raccoon dogs." (I've never seen a raccoon dog, and I'm not sure I want to.)

This is pretty brazen, when you think about it. Customers are making a conscious choice to take a stand against animal cruelty, and yet they're buying real fur without even knowing it. This would be like buying a veggie burger at a restaurant, and then later finding out you're eating a hamburger. The head of the fur-free campaign for The Humane Society of the United States, Pierre Grzybowski, calls it an "outrageous deception."

So why are these companies even bothering with the bait and switch?

"Well, actually, some of the good faux furs can be more expensive to use when making jackets or other garments than low-quality animal fur," explains Grzybowski. "They may use animal fur just because it's cheaper." That's right, the fake stuff can often be more expensive than the real stuff!

The good news is that our investigation did score some immediate results. One store removed black designer boots that were fake-fake. Others offered full refunds to anyone who was concerned they had unknowingly purchased real fur.

My only one remaining question is this: Why couldn't this have happened with cubic zirconia? [Sigh.] Maybe one day . . .

9

A SHOCKING CONCLUSION

EVERY ONCE IN A WHILE, the Rossen Reports team will do an investigation that, to put it scientifically, shocks the hell out of us. Sometimes literally (like stray voltage), sometimes figuratively (could I walk through fire?), and we were especially shocked by what we learned with tire repair vendors.

- ◎ Getting Zapped: Hidden Danger on Your Block
- ◎ How to Walk Through Fire (I Did It)
- ◎ The Happy Ending

Getting Zapped: Hidden
Danger on Your Block

We do it every single day. We walk down the street and we touch harmless things such as lamps, fences, signs, and lampposts. We don't think twice about it. But what would happen if these common everyday objects were secretly electrified, and simply touching them would send shock waves through your body? It sounds like the plot of an evil villain from a bad Batman movie—"I will *electrify* Gotham City, muhahaha!"—but it's actually happening, and it's happening more often than you'd think.

"This is a serious safety hazard," says Dave Kalokitis, chief engineer at Power Survey, a no-nonsense, straight-talking engineer with a mustache and a yellow hard hat. "Sidewalks, manhole covers, roadways, fences, anything that's in our landscape that has wires buried underground. When they fail, they'll leak to the surface."

It's called stray voltage, and this invisible killer comes from cities with old infrastructure, old wires that have eroded and frayed. When the insulation is frayed, the voltage leaks out . . . and that voltage can linger on ordinary surfaces. If you touch it, you fry.

"When a water system breaks down, you see a puddle. Electricity—there's no telltale," explains Kalokitis.

And that's the scariest part. There's no way to tell just by looking at it, which is why, across the country, children and pets have been shocked and killed. To get a better handle on this danger, Kalokitis and a team of engineers take me on an electric tour of Washington, D.C., and they scan some ordinary-looking objects for stray voltage. As they point their electric gizmos at sidewalks and street signs, it's the closest I've ever come to being in a *Ghostbusters* movie—all we need is a proton pack.

Kalokitis points at a streetlight—looks harmless. "We've identified voltage on this streetlight," he says, looking at his sensors. "And when I take this household light bulb and make contact to it, the light bulb lights up." And, sure enough, without being plugged in, when the light bulb just *touches* the lamppost, it begins to glow. I can't believe my eyes. This looks like a normal lamppost lighting up a bulb.

"That's scary," I say.

"Absolutely scary. And it could be deadly."

For his next trick, Kalokitis grounds a screwdriver, and then he holds it next to the same innocent-looking lamppost. Sparks fly from the post, streaking through the dark sky. It's the same kind of post that you might casually lean against, say, when waiting for a bus. The stray voltage is so powerful, in fact, that Kalokitis radios the problem in to the city. Then he tests more streetlights—more stray voltage. It's everywhere. Even the *sidewalk* is secretly electrified.

"The sidewalk has ninety volts on it," Kalokitis says, showing me the electrical reader.

"If this is so common, why aren't people dying from this every single day?" I ask.

"Well, a couple of things have to happen to get a shock. You have to touch it. And then if your feet are wet, it's particularly dangerous."

So there's an important safety tip: Never, um, get your feet wet? Never touch anything? It's an admittedly frustrating danger that we are mostly powerless to avoid.

The stray voltage is everywhere—even on a bus sign that is *not* connected to any wires. Kalokitis's Ghostbusters-looking sensors tell him that this sign, too, is buzzing with secret electricity. How is that possible? Because there are wires underground, and the pole is driven into the wires.

In just that one night, our team of engineers found more than forty locations with stray voltage. "It's a very reactive situation," warns Kalokitis, meaning that "usually *after* there is a death or an injury, there's testing. But prior to that, nothing happens."

And it's also a danger that, for some reason, seems especially hazardous for pets. Why do puppies and kittens keep getting zapped?

"Well, pets don't have the protection of shoes," explains Kalokitis. "So their bare paws are touching the ground, and electricity can pass right through their body."

Experts say that less than 2 percent of cities are proactively testing for stray voltage. That means that, in all likelihood, on your very street, stray voltage could be hidden in the metal fences, in the streetlights, or anywhere there is metal.

TAKEAWAY: Experts say the best advice is to not touch metal objects on the street unless you have to, and if you do get shocked, report it to your utility so they come and fix it.

The whole thing is, well, shocking.

How to Walk Through Fire (I Did It)

For years, motivational gurus have inspired future CEOs, business leaders, and millionaires by walking on hot coals with their bare feet. *Mind over matter,* the saying goes, and if you can conquer the burning embers with nothing but your iron will, then you can dominate your competition or make billions of dollars or unleash your inner Steve Jobs. (Or something.)

Sometimes, though, people get hurt. In a well-publicized PR fiasco, for example, disciples of Tony Robbins tried to walk over the hot coals, and instead of landing on the cover of *Fortune* magazine, they landed in the emergency room. (The Tony Robbins people said "only 5 of 7,000 participants requested any examination beyond what was readily available on-site.")

The hot coals ritual has been around for decades and it will be around for decades more, so I had to know . . . how dangerous is this, really? Is it something that I could recommend to a friend in good conscience? And sure, maybe part of me also wondered . . . *do I have what it takes?*

I traveled to Ithaca, New York, for a session with a group called LifeCourage, which holds motivational seminars that include fire walking. Now, according to the gurus, walking over coals is about things like "transforming your life" and "conquering your fears," and perhaps that's true, but before I risked setting my toes on fire, I wanted to do one very simple thing: practice.

"You want to step lightly, but walk briskly," says Dr. Robert Glatter, who works at the Lenox Hill Hospital emergency room. He advises me not to run. "When you run, you actually have *more* contact with your feet on the hot coals, and then you could risk having a burn."

Got it. So the night before the big event, in my hotel room, I practiced walking over hot coals. Wait, that actually makes it sound cooler than it really was; let me rephrase that—in my hotel room, *I practiced walking.* When's the last time you practiced walking? I thought deeply about the doctor's instructions to walk "evenly but briskly." So in my hotel room, I literally walked from the door to the bed, evenly and briskly, back and forth, again and again. Door to bed. Bed to door. I'm now a champion room walker. If you ever need someone to walk from a bed to a door, I'm your man.

The next morning, confident in my walking abilities, I speak with Tony Simons, from LifeCourage. I decide to address the elephant in the room.

"The critics say that this is just hocus-pocus, that this is a way to get people into these motivational seminars, to pay money. And it's really got nothing to do with spirituality or mentalism; it's got to do with science, physics, that's it."

"Right," says Tony.

"What do you say to that?"

He pauses for a second. It's no doubt a question he's heard before. "Of course it's physics. Everything is physics. . . . The reason why people do it is because it helps them stay focused, it gives people access to more courage, which is useful in life as you face a scary, daunting situation, and you stay focused and relaxed and thoughtful in approaching that."

That's a fair response. In other words, it's a way for people to go through life and say, *If I've walked through fire, I can handle whatever challenge.*

"And it makes people realize how powerful they are," Tony adds.

It's almost time for my walk across fire, but first, I join about fifteen other fire walkers in an hourlong session where we sit in a semicircle and talk about our feelings. I didn't know quite what to expect. I was never the kind of guy who attended conferences that preached motivational slogans like *The Power of Positive Thinking!*, so I wondered who, exactly, are the kind of people who desire to walk on hot coals? Are they cultists? Kooks? Or are they just ordinary people looking for an outlet to have a better life?

As I sit cross-legged and gaze around the semicircle, I realize . . . they're looking at me and thinking the same thing. Maybe *I'm* the kooky one. After all, I'm the guy who buried myself alive, stranded myself in the ocean, and investigated used women's underwear. I suppose we're all just different shades of kook.

After an hour of the semicircle warm and fuzzies, it's time for me to channel my inner Khaleesi and attempt to walk through fire. Now, there are three things you should know about walking on hot coals. The first is that the charcoal is indeed hot; after they're lit on fire, the charcoal itself is 1,000 degrees. This would melt your bones.

Yet here's the second thing: Those coals are covered with a thin layer of ash, and the ash is cooler than what's burning below, much cooler, and the ash protects your feet from the scalding embers.

The third thing? "Mental preparation will *not* help you get across more safely," counsels Dr. Glatter. "It's pure physics. It's not mind over matter."

Oddly, I found that advice somehow comforting. Pure physics. I try to remember this as I approach the start of the coals, staring at the orange embers smoldering on the ground. Nearby, an ambulance and a team of paramedics are on standby, just in case.

I won't lie to you: I'm nervous as hell. And let's be honest, I'm doing this live, on national TV, mic'd up and relaying all of this to Matt Lauer and Savannah Guthrie. What if I wuss out? What if I start doing the chicken dance?

In near darkness, I can feel the heat of the embers. My body begins to sweat. I ask Tony, the guru, if he has any final words of advice.

"I want you to walk with your palms up," Tony says.

"Okay." I extend my arms out to the sides and keep my palms up, as this either appeases the Gods of Fire or helps with balance—one of the two.

"I want you to unclench your bottom," Tony says.

"Okay," I say, and try not to bust up laughing.

"Stay loose," Tony says, soothingly. "Breathe deep. And when the group is going to start chanting, I want you to listen to the song of the group, I want you to imagine the song carrying you safely through the fire."

"Okay," and then I can't help but ask him, "What is it going to feel like when I first walk on it? I'm nervous."

"It might feel like you're stepping onto a bed of popcorn, it might feel hot," Tony says, and I wonder . . . who has ever stepped on a bed of popcorn? Tony continues, "In either case, I want you to stay focused. I want you to stay relaxed."

I try to focus. I try to relax. Yet I'll admit that, well, my butt is not unclenched.

I raise my arms, keep my palms up, and try to remember the advice from the expert—even steps, brisk, light.

"Yes, yes, yes, yes." Tony begins to chant. Then the groups starts chanting.

I take my first step. It's hot but I don't freak out—second step, third step—*brisk, light, even*—bed to door, door to bed, bed to door, fourth step, fifth step, and before I even know it . . . Done!

"Oh, it's hot," I say, and it *is* hot but, to be honest, it's not nearly as hot as you would imagine. My feet are pretty gross for morning

TV—they're as black as tar, and it will take a lot of scrubbing to get them clean, but they are not burnt or blistered. It feels a lot like walking over really, really hot sand on the beach. At some point in your life, you've probably walked on sand this hot.

For some people, facing the challenge of the burning coals—and then conquering this challenge—really *does* give a motivational jolt, and it offers proof that you can summon strength you didn't know you had. And, hey, if that floats their boat, great. But for me, well, it really just felt like walking over very hot sand.

"Wow, it feels really hot," I report back to the NBC anchors in New York, "but I have no burns."

"How do you feel?" Savannah Guthrie asks me.

"I'm okay, I'm okay, no need for the paramedics, luckily."

"Jeff, ask the expert," Savannah says, a little slyly, "can you re-clench your bottom now?"

The Happy Ending

And now it's time for something truly shocking, as if you haven't already been shocked enough.

We've seen fishy business when it comes to auto repairs, but this one really threw us for a loop. We're talking about tires. When it gets cold outside, the air pressure in tires drops. When that happens, a little warning light starts flashing on your dashboard.

The fix? It's easy—just add some air. Done and done.

But would repair shops do the right thing? Or would they upsell you with countless repairs that you don't really need, like Puddy did?

To investigate, we hatched an experiment that should, by now, be quite familiar to you: We took a normal, healthy, 2010 Chrysler minivan and we hired a certified mechanic, Audra Fordin, to inspect every square inch.

She gives it a full inspection, then pronounces: "The car's in perfect condition. It needs nothing."

Then we have her rig a simple problem.

"We are going to let some air out of the tires, trigger that dashboard light to come on," says Audra.

Hissssssss . . . the tires deflate.

"What's the fix?" I ask.

"The fix is free air. Period."

Okay, but let's see what the repair shops say. Just like old times, we send our producer Jovanna to go undercover and see what they would charge, driving from car dealers to national chains to independent garages.

"I have this light that came on in my car," Jovanna says to the first repairman, feigning a note of confusion. "I'm not really sure what it is."

The dealer inspects the car. "All you have to do is just go to a gas station and put air in it, and drive, and the light will go out. That's it."

The dealer doesn't charge us a dime. Okay, so far so good, but would we be as lucky at the big chain stores?

We visit a national chain. The repairman inspects the car. "You don't need to fix anything. It was just low on air."

Huh. We hear that again, and again, and *again*. At another national chain, the shop even removes Jovanna's tire to inspect it for leaks. (So thorough! So honest!) One repairman even gives Jovanna a bit of solid life advice. "Don't tell the mechanic you don't know anything," he advises. "He's going to rip you off. We are not like that."

A SHOCKING CONCLUSION

It turns out that *no one* was like that. The car dealerships. The national chains. The independent garages—none of them overcharged. In the end, everyone did the right thing. This is a Rossen Reports first. Miracles do happen.

I almost didn't include this in the book—it's like a magic trick with no trick—but it does hit home an important point: Not *all* of the world is out to get you. Not every retailer is peddling false goods. Not every contractor is a hustler. It's important to keep your guard up—that's what this book is all about—but it's also important to remember that life has plenty of good guys.

PARTING THOUGHTS

YOU MADE IT. THANKS FOR hanging in there.

This is going to sound weird, but I hope that you never have to use most of what you just read in this book. I hope that you never get hustled by a mechanic or get zapped by stray voltage.

On the other hand, I also hope that the lessons in this book help you conquer the challenges that you *will* someday face. Some are inevitable. Most of us buy things online—now you know a few tricks to ensure that what you're buying is legit. All of us know someone who's at risk of a heart attack—now you know what to do. All of us travel, all of us ride in cars, and all of us go to doctors—now you know how to protect yourself.

Just remember that in all of these topics—from tornadoes to web-cam predators to counterfeit prom gowns—you don't have to be an *expert*. You just need to know a few basic things and ask a few basic questions. The next time it's late at night and you're exhausted and you're thinking about driving home, I hope you'll let someone else take the wheel. The next time you go shopping for a dishwasher or a TV, I hope you remember to negotiate. The next time you buckle your kid's seat belt, make sure they're not wearing a winter coat. And the next time you go on an "all-inclusive" vacation in paradise, well . . . call me! I'm happy to be your guest.

Until then,

Jeff Rossen

ACKNOWLEDGMENTS

So many people to thank. I'll keep it moving so the Oscars people don't play me off the stage.

I couldn't do any of this without my amazing family, as Danielle and the kids sacrifice so much so I can travel and do this work. They're the real heroes. (Thanks again, Skyler, Sloane, and Blake.) Of course, huge hugs and kisses to my parents, who have supported this wild ride since I was a little boy—even when it seemed impossible. They always encouraged me to follow my dreams. Mom and Dad, we did it!

Then there's my work family. My producers. I love each and every one of them—past and present—including Robert Powell, who helped kick-start this adventure several years ago, along with super-agent Olivia Metzger at CAA. An especially big thanks to Jovanna Billington, Lindsey Bomnin, Anneke Foster, and Kathryn Nathanson—all solid gold. My tireless behind-the-scenes team doesn't get nearly enough credit for flying all over, spending time away from their loved ones, and doing the impossible: dealing with me and my pie-in-the-sky ideas. They always make it happen. I'm eternally grateful.

Josh Davis, my Jedi. Josh runs the Rossen Reports unit, and my life. He also played a huge role in this book—helping to craft the look, the content, not to mention the countless hours reading, rereading, and rereading again. Josh, I couldn't do it without you. Thank you!

When I first decided to write this book (my first), I didn't know what to expect. The fantastic team at Flatiron immediately put me at ease—from my first meeting with Bob Miller, president of Flatiron, to months and months of editing with the indefatigable editorial team of Will Schwalbe and Bryn Clark. Special thanks to VP Liz Keenan, Nancy Trypuc and Molly Fonseca in marketing, Steven Boriack in publicity, and Elizabeth Much from E2W Collective, Keith Hayes who directed the cover, Deborah Feingold who photographed me for the cover, Phil Pascuzzo who designed the jacket and illustrations, and Richard Oriolo, the interior designer. You are all the best in the business, and I've learned so much. Side note: I thought the television industry was odd . . . until I got a peek at publishing. (Maybe that's why I felt right at home from beginning to end.)

My collaborator Jeff Wilser. We hit it off from minute one. Jeff, your wisdom, attention to detail, literary prowess, and passion for your work made this experience unforgettable. Plus, you're a super cool guy.

Many thanks to my bosses at NBC, including Jim Bell and Steve Capus, who made the bold decision to form this unit back in 2012. Soon Deborah Turness and Rich Esposito would take the reins, and take our work to new heights. We couldn't do any of it without our superb investigative leaders Richard Greenberg and Robert Dembo—not to mention the stellar legal advice of Steve Chung (he's quite funny, too . . . for a lawyer) and legal dynamo Susan Weiner. A huge thanks to the executives in the front office who continue to support me, led by the chairman of NBC News and MSNBC, Andy Lack, and NBC News president Noah Oppenheim. Of course, thanks to everyone at *Today*, including executive producer Don Nash and co-executive producer Tom Mazzarelli, who always provide the resources we need to tell these important stories in new and unique ways.

Thanks to the experts, doctors, scientists, and survivalists who provide us with vital life-saving information. These men and women work hard every day to keep us safe. I personally appreciate the time they give us to help amplify their messages.

And finally . . . thank YOU . . . for inviting me into your home each morning, and now, letting me sit on your coffee table. We're in this together. Let's keep going!

INDEX

INDEX

INDEX